ASIAN WATER DEVELOPMENT OUTLOOK 2016

DESCRIPTION OF METHODOLOGY AND DATA

ASIAN DEVELOPMENT BANK

© 2017 Asian Development Bank
6 ADB Avenue, Mandaluyong City, 1550 Metro Manila, Philippines
Tel +63 2 632 4444; Fax +63 2 636 2444
www.adb.org

Some rights reserved. Published in 2017.
Printed in the Philippines.

ISBN 978-92-9257-729-2 (Print), 978-92-9257-730-8 (e-ISBN)
Publication Stock No. RPT178628-2
DOI: http://dx.doi.org/10.22617/RPT178628-2

Cataloging-In-Publication Data

Asian Development Bank.
        Asian water development outlook 2016: Description of methodology and data.
Mandaluyong City, Philippines: Asian Development Bank, 2017.

1. Water.   2. Water security index.   3. Water governance.   I. Asian Development Bank.

Notes:
In this publication, "$" refers to US dollars.
Corrigenda to ADB publications may be found at http://www.adb.org/publications/corrigenda

Printed on recycled paper

Contents

Tables and Figures

Tables

Figures

Acknowledgments

The Asian Development Bank (ADB) thanks authors Yasmin Siddiqi (ADB) and Eelco van Beek (Technical Committee, Global Water Partnership) for preparing the methodology report to supplement the Asian Water Development Outlook 2016.

ADB also thanks the following authors for their rigorous preparation of the individual reports for each Key Dimension (KD):

- KD 1—Household Water Security: Fu Sun, Asia Pacifi c Center for Water Security, Tsinghua University
- KD2—Economic Water Security: Jonathan Lautze, Herath Manthrithilake, David Wiberg, Bunyod Holmatov (consultant), and Anil Terway (consultant), International Water Management Institute
- KD3—Urban Water Security: Eva Abal, Kris Fox, Steve Kenway, and Ka Leung Lam, International Water Center
- KD4—Environmental Water Security: Stuart Bunn and Ben Stewart-Koster, Australian Rivers Institute, Griffith University, and International Water Center; Günther Fisher, International Institute for Applied Systems Analysis; Pamela Green, City College of New York; and David Wiberg, International Water Management Institute
- KD5—Resilience to Water-Related Disasters: Ian Makin, International Water Management Institute; Narciso Prudente (consultant), ADB; and Eelco van Beek, Technical Committee, Global Water Partnership

Abbreviations

ADB	Asian Development Bank
APCWS	Asia-Pacific Center for Water Security – Tsinghua University
AWDO	Asian Water Development Outlook
DALYs	disability-adjusted life years
EO	Expert Opinion
ESCAP	Economic and Social Commission for Asia and the Pacific
GDP	gross domestic product
GWP	Global Water Partnership
IWC	International Water Center
IWMI	International Water Management Institute
JMP	Joint Monitoring Programme (WHO/UNICEF)
KD	key dimension
NWS	National Water Security
NWSI	National Water Security Index
OECD	Organisation for Economic Co-operation and Development
UNICEF	United Nations Children's Emergency Fund
WHO	World Health Organization

1 Introduction

This document provides background information on the applied methodology and the underlying data of the Asian Water Development Outlook 2016 (AWDO 2016). The purpose is to document the methodology and the data and to answer questions interested parties might have on the background of the results of AWDO 2016.

The methodology used for AWDO 2016 has been developed by reputed scientific institutes and has been subject to quality control standards with respect to the approach followed, assumptions made, and the data used. Where reliable data were lacking, expert opinions were used to determine the scores. As much as possible, generally accessible and maintained databases (United Nations [UN], World Bank, Asian Development Bank [ADB], universities, etc.) have been used. How such databases were populated or how the data were sourced was beyond our control and quality assurance or quality control process.

AWDO integrates the many dimensions of water security and applies it at a national scale. Combining, for example, pure statistical economic information with governance indices required many simplifying assumptions to be made. It will not be difficult to question some of these assumptions and the data that were used. Questions can also be asked about the validity of the country-level results knowing that there are huge regional differences within these countries. These questions are very valid. Still, we are convinced that the results make sense and that they indicate where progress can be made by the countries on how to improve water security. The results enable comparisons between countries and regions. Given the uncertainties involved, however, no absolute value should be given to the actual scores. The scores can easily be 10% higher or lower than what is presented in AWDO 2016. However, this will not change the message that AWDO 2016 conveys. We are confident that the methodology is useful for our nonparametric approach using data to determine scores rather than rely on absolute values.

The structure of this document is as follows. Chapter 2 gives the background and underlying vision of the AWDO approach. Chapter 3 provides an overview of the overall methodological approach and how we dealt with missing data. That chapter should be seen as an introduction of the subsequent five chapters (Chapters 4–8) in which the approach is described for all five key dimensions. For each key dimension, the overall assessment framework for that key dimension will be described, followed by a description of the subindicators (including data used, changes compared with AWDO 2013, and missing data). Chapter 9 describes how the National Water Security Index as well as the national water security level are determined. Finally, Chapter 10 gives a general assessment of the approach and recommendations on how to continue the AWDO process. Additional information and data are given in the appendixes. In particular, Appendix 3 is important as it contains the underlying data and provides a comparison with AWDO 2013.

This methodology report includes a compilation of the reports written by the key dimension teams for AWDO 2016. For additional and more detailed information on the five key dimensions (KD 1–5), reference is made to their reports.

2 The Vision behind the Asian Water Development Outlook Methodological Approach

2.1 Defining Water Security

The meaning and definition of the term "water security" has developed over time. While in the 1990s the term was mostly used to express a general vision, in the past 10 years it has increasingly been used to make explicit the goals explicit that we want to achieve with better management. This requires definitions of what water security is and how we can measure water security. An overview of these developments and use of water security in water management is given in van Beek and Lincklaen Arriens (2014).

Many definitions of water security exist and most have a certain sector bias. The following definitions are the most comprehensive and most referenced:

1. "The reliable availability of an acceptable quantity and quality of water for production, livelihoods and health, coupled with an acceptable level of risk to society of unpredictable water-related impacts" (Grey and Sadoff 2007).
2. "The capacity of a population to safeguard sustainable access to adequate quantities of acceptable quality water for sustaining livelihoods, human well-being, and socio-economic development, for ensuring protection against water-borne pollution and water-related disasters, and for preserving ecosystems in a climate of peace and political stability" (UNU 2013).

The concept of water security is still developing. The current thinking is largely focused on infrastructure. While the importance of infrastructure is confirmed in the GWP/OECD report Securing Water, Sustaining Growth (Sadoff et al. 2015), the report also mentions the need to make water security more risk and opportunity oriented.

2.2 Vision of Water Security

In developing the analytical framework for AWDO 2013, the following shared vision of water security was formulated:

> Societies can enjoy water security when they successfully manage their water resources and services to
>
> 1. satisfy household water and sanitation needs in all communities;
> 2. support productive economies in agriculture, industry, and energy;
> 3. develop vibrant, livable cities and towns;
> 4. restore healthy rivers and ecosystems; and
> 5. build resilient communities that can adapt to change.

To quantify water security, this vision was developed into a water security framework with five interdependent key dimensions. These key dimensions are illustrated in Figure 1 and are described in more detail in the next section.

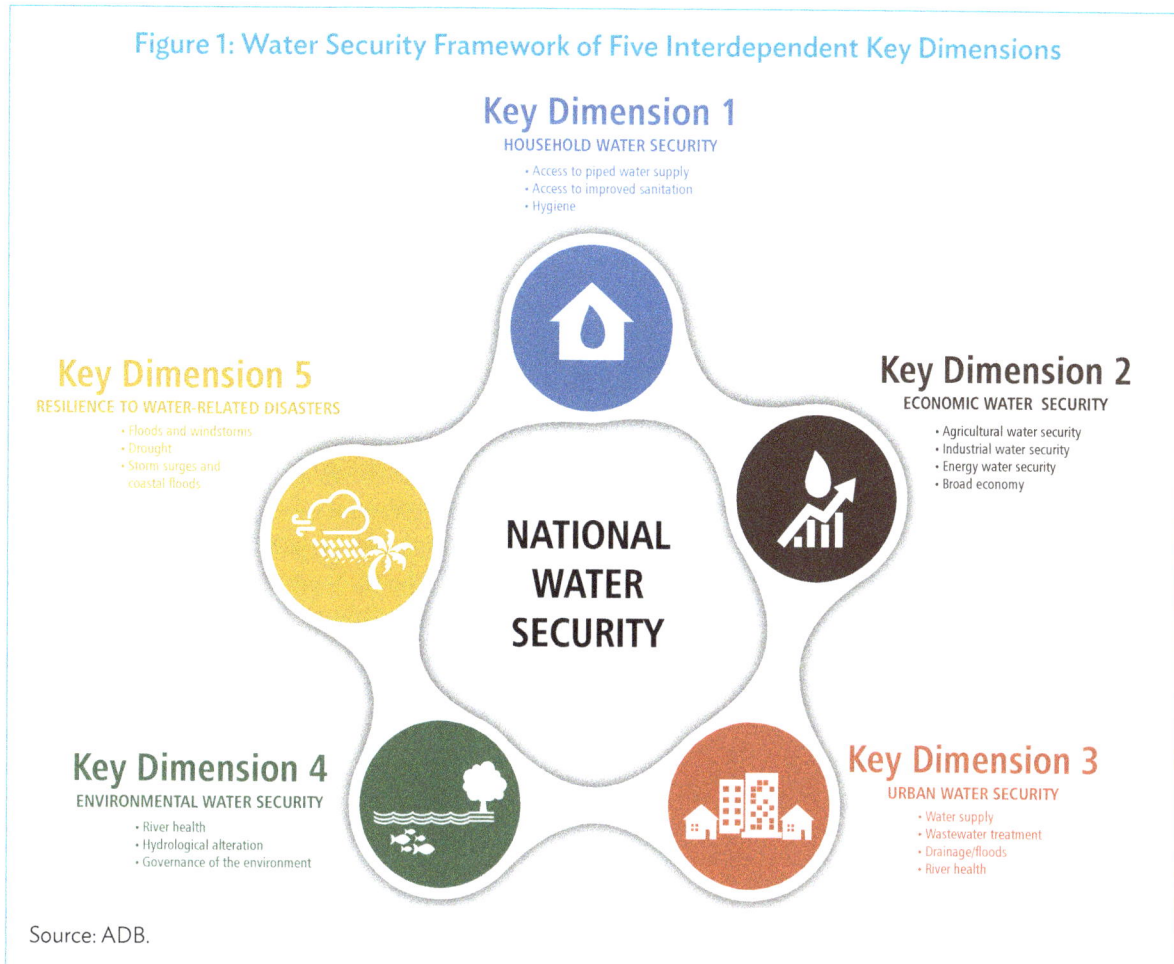

Figure 1: Water Security Framework of Five Interdependent Key Dimensions

Key Dimension 1
HOUSEHOLD WATER SECURITY
- Access to piped water supply
- Access to improved sanitation
- Hygiene

Key Dimension 5
RESILIENCE TO WATER-RELATED DISASTERS
- Floods and windstorms
- Drought
- Storm surges and coastal floods

Key Dimension 2
ECONOMIC WATER SECURITY
- Agricultural water security
- Industrial water security
- Energy water security
- Broad economy

NATIONAL WATER SECURITY

Key Dimension 4
ENVIRONMENTAL WATER SECURITY
- River health
- Hydrological alteration
- Governance of the environment

Key Dimension 3
URBAN WATER SECURITY
- Water supply
- Wastewater treatment
- Drainage/floods
- River health

Source: ADB.

2.3 Key Dimensions of Water Security

Key Dimension 1: Household Water Security

The foundation and cornerstone of water security is what happens at the household level. Providing all people with reliable, safe water and sanitation services should be the top priority of Asia's leaders. Household water security is an essential foundation for efforts to eradicate poverty and support economic development.

Key Dimension 2: Economic Water Security

Water grows our food, powers our industry, and cools our energy-generating plants. The use of water in these sectors must no longer be seen in isolation from each other. Debate about the water–food–energy nexus has begun to raise general awareness about the critical interaction among water uses to support economic activities. Economic water security measures the productive use of water to sustain economic growth in the food production, industry, and energy sectors of the economy.

Key Dimension 3: Urban Water Security
In Asia and the Pacific, about 48% of the population currently lives in urban areas; however, the urban proportion has risen by 29% over the past 20 years, more rapidly than in any other region. After a century of transformation from agrarian rural societies to urban centers and the creation of the world's largest number of megacities, Asia's cities have become important drivers of the economy. The urban water security indicators measure the creation of better water management and services to support vibrant and livable water-sensitive cities.

Key Dimension 4: Environmental Water Security
Asia's environment and precious natural resources have suffered greatly from decades of neglect as governments across the region prioritized rapid economic growth over environmental objectives. Asia's leaders are now starting to green their economies as a broader focus on sustainable development and inclusive growth gains ground. The environmental water security indicator assesses the health of rivers and measures progress on restoring rivers and ecosystems to health on a national and regional scale. The sustainability of development and improved lives depends on these natural resources.

Key Dimension 5: Resilience to Water-Related Disasters
The region's growing prosperity has involved unprecedented changes in economic activity, urbanization, diets, trade, culture, and communication. It has also brought increasing levels of uncertainty and risk from climate variability and change. The resilience of communities in Asia and the Pacific to these changes, and especially to water-related disaster risks, is assessed with the indicator of resilience to water-related disasters. The building of resilient communities that can adapt to change and are able to reduce risk from natural disasters related to water must be accelerated to minimize the impact of future disasters.

2.4 National Water Security

The overall national water security (NWS) of each country is assessed as the composite result of the five key dimensions, measured on a scale of 1–5. The pentagram of water security (Figure 1) illustrates that the dimensions of water security are related and interdependent, and should not be treated in isolation of each other.

AWDO measures water security by quantifying the five key dimensions in terms of clear and measurable indicators. Table 1 describes all five key dimensions, what is measured, and which measurable indicators are used. In the next chapter, a detailed description will be given how the key dimensions are quantified.

The interdependence of the factors that determine water security in each dimension means that increases in water security will be achieved by governments that "break the traditional sector silos" to find ways and means to manage the linkages, synergies, and trade-offs among the dimensions. This is the process known as integrated water resources management, which was adopted by world leaders in Johannesburg in 2002 at the World Summit on Sustainable Development and which was reaffirmed at the UN Conference on Sustainable Development Rio+20 Summit in 2012.

The descriptions of the five stages of the national water security assessment are summarized in Table 2. At National Water Security Index (NWSI) 1, the NWS situation is hazardous and there is a large gap between the current state and the acceptable levels of water security. At NWSI 5, the country may be considered a model for its management of water services and water resources, and the country is as water-secure as possible under current circumstances.

Table 1: Asian Water Development Outlook Framework Assessing National Water Security

Key Dimension	Index	What the Index Measures	What the Index Is Composed of
National Water Security	National water security	How far countries have progressed toward national water security	Combination of the five dimensions of water security measured by the key dimensions
Key Dimension 1 (KD1)	Household water security	To what extent countries are satisfying their household water and sanitation needs and improving hygiene for public health	• Access to piped water supply • Access to improved sanitation • Hygiene index (measured in disability-adjusted life years, DALYs)
Key Dimension 2 (KD2)	Economic water security	The productive use of water to sustain economic growth in food production, industry, and energy	• Broad economic development • Water for agriculture • Water for industry • Water for energy
Key Dimension 3 (KD3)	Urban water security	Progress toward better urban water services and management to develop vibrant, livable cities and towns	• Urban water supply • Urban wastewater collection • Flood and storm drainage • Urban river health
Key Dimension 4 (KD4)	Environmental water security	How well river basins are being managed to sustain ecosystem services	• River health • Flow alteration • Environmental governance
Key Dimension 5 (KD5)	Resilience to water-related disasters	The capacity to cope with and recover from the impacts of water-related disasters	• Floods and windstorms • Droughts • Storm surges and coastal floods

Source: ADB.

2.5 The Regions

The calculations are primarily done and presented at the country level. For presentation and comparison purposes, regional summaries are provided. The regions identified follow those of ADB and are given in Table 3. The total population (2014) considered in AWDO 2016 is 4.044 trillion. Note that Pakistan is included in the region Central and West Asia and not in South Asia, and also that compared with AWDO 2013 Niue is no longer considered. The regional scores given in the next chapters are population-weighted averages. This means that the score of East Asia as a region is strongly determined by the People's Republic of China's score and the score of South Asia (to a somewhat lesser extent) by India's score. The Pacific region contains only 0.3% of the total population in Asia and the Pacific.

Table 2: Description of National Water Security Stages

NWS Index	NWS Score	NWS Stage	Description
5	96 and above	Model	All people have access to safe drinking water and sanitation facilities; economic activities are not constrained by water availability; water quality meets standards for people and ecology; and water-related risks are acceptable and relatively easy to deal with.
4	76<96	Effective	Nearly all people have access to safe drinking water and sanitation facilities; water service delivery is mostly formal and effective to support economic development; water quality is in general acceptable and attention is given to ecological restoration of water bodies; and water-related risks are seriously brought down by infrastructure and warning systems.
3	56<76	Capable	Access to safe drinking water and sanitation facilities is further improving, also in rural and poor areas; water productivity in economic activities has improved; water quality is improving through regulation and wastewater treatment; first measures are taken to restore ecological health of the water bodies; and the most serious water-related risks are being addressed.
2	36<56	Engaged	More than half the people have access to modest drinking water and sanitation facilities; water service delivery is starting to develop, supporting economic activities; first measures are taken to improve water quality; and first attempts are being made to address water-related risks.
1	0<36	Hazardous	Drinking water and sanitation facilities are limited and impose serious health risks; water service delivery is mostly informal and a constraining factor for economic activities and development; water quality is poor and dangerous for people; serious damage to aquatic ecology is present; and droughts and floods drive people into poverty.

NWS = national water security.
Source: ADB.

Table 3: Regions Identified for the Asian Water Development Outlook 2016 and Their Population

Region	Economies	Total Population in 2014 (million)
Central and West Asia	Afghanistan, Armenia, Azerbaijan, Georgia, Kazakhstan, Kyrgyz Republic, Pakistan, Tajikistan, Turkmenistan, and Uzbekistan	299 (7%)
East Asia	People's Republic of China; Mongolia; and Taipei,China	1,420 (35%)
Pacific	Cook Islands, Federated States of Micronesia, Fiji, Kiribati, Marshall Islands, Nauru, Palau, Papua New Guinea, Samoa, Solomon Islands, Timor-Leste, Tonga, Tuvalu, and Vanuatu	11 (0.3%)
South Asia	Bangladesh, Bhutan, India, Maldives, Nepal, and Sri Lanka	1,477 (37%)
Southeast Asia	Cambodia, Indonesia, Lao People's Democratic Republic, Malaysia, Myanmar, Philippines, Thailand, and Viet Nam	619 (15%)
Advanced Economies	Australia; Brunei Darussalam; Hong Kong, China; Japan; New Zealand; Republic of Korea; and Singapore	218 (5%)
Total (Asia and the Pacific)		**4,044 (100%)**

Note: Given that the total global population in 2014 was 7.266 trillion, AWDO 2016 addresses 56% of the global population.
Source: Derived from Appendix 1.

3 Methodological Approach

3.1 Scoring Approach

AWDO distinguishes four levels of indicators. The highest level is the National Water Security Index (NWSI). The NWS score is composed by combining the scores of the key dimensions 1–5. Each key dimension score in turn is the result of a combination of the scores of several subindicators. Most subindicators are again determined by combining the scores of sub-subindicators. Figure 2 illustrates this process: sub-subindicators provide the information to determine the scores of the subindicators. The subindicators together determine the scores of the key dimensions (the actual indicators), usually by just summing the results of the subindicators. Finally, the NWSI is the sum of the key dimension scores.

For each key dimension, a specific scoring approach has been developed. This will be explained in the description of the key dimensions. The ultimate resulting score of each key dimension is normalized

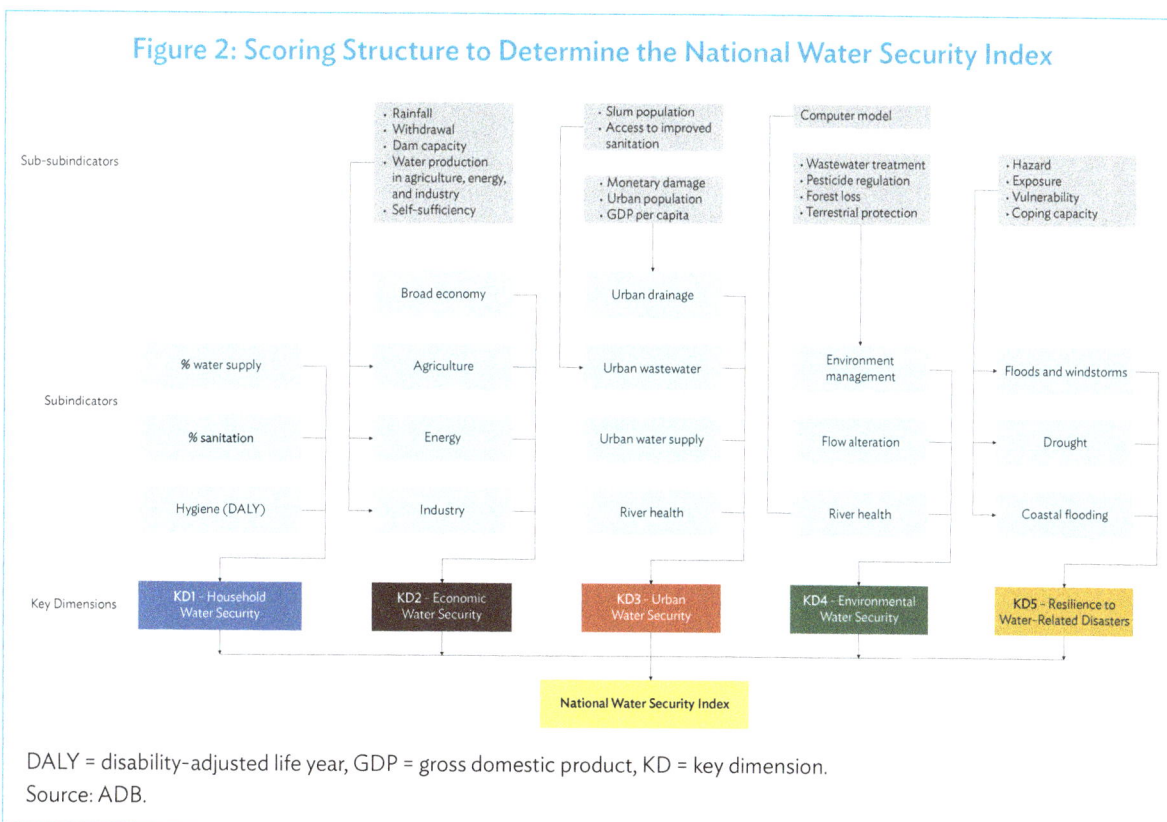

Figure 2: Scoring Structure to Determine the National Water Security Index

DALY = disability-adjusted life year, GDP = gross domestic product, KD = key dimension.
Source: ADB.

to a maximum of 20. The score for the NWSI is simply the sum of the scores of the five key dimensions. Hence, the maximum score for the NWSI is 100. The scoring of the NWSI and the NWS level will be described in more detail in Chapter 9.

Besides the NWS scores, AWDO 2016 also assigns development stages to the NWS situation and the key dimensions. The development stages for the NWS is given in Table 2 and are expressed on a five-point scale with NWSI 1 standing for "hazardous" and NWSI 5 for "model." Indices for the key dimensions are assigned in a similar manner, though based on a scale of 1–20. An overview of this banding is given in Chapter 9 (Table 40).

3.2 Data Sources Used and Year of Origin

As much as possible, publicly available trusted databases that are regularly updated have been used for AWDO 2016, such as ones from UN agencies, World Bank, and ADB. Which databases have been used is described in the chapters on the key dimensions. An overview of all data sources used for AWDO 2016 is given in Appendix 5.

Although the year 2016 in the title AWDO 2016 might give the impression that the document describes the situation of 2016, the documents actually report analyses carried out in 2015, using the most recent data available at that time. In general, this will be published data of 2015 and earlier. The raw data collection may have been (or is likely to have been) earlier than the published year. Information of the years of publication of the data and the actual "raw data" years will be given in the descriptions of the key dimensions and in Appendix 5. Table 4 provides an overview of these publication years for AWDO 2016 as well as for AWDO 2013.

As a general rule of thumb, one might consider that AWDO 2016 describes the situation in 2014 while AWDO 2013 (due to a long publishing process) described the situation in 2009. Hence, comparing AWDO 2016 with AWDO 2013 will show the progress made in 5 years.

3.3 Dealing with Missing Data

The data used in AWDO 2016 mostly come from well-maintained formal databases. Appendix 5 gives

Table 4: Years of Publication of the Data Used in the Asian Water Development Outlook

	Asian Water Development Outlook 2013	Asian Water Development Outlook 2016
Key Dimension 1	JMP 2009; DALY 2004	JMP 2014; DALY 2012
Key Dimension 2	2007–2009	2012–2013
Key Dimension 3	2009/10	2015
Key Dimension 4	2000	2012–2014
Key Dimension 5	2005–2009	2012–2015

DALY = disability-adjusted life year, JMP = Joint Monitoring Programme.
Source: ADB.

an overview of the databases used. In case these databases did not contain data for certain indicators for certain countries, the following procedure was followed:

- First, an attempt was made to find the data from other data sources, preferably from formal (other) databases, but otherwise from referenced literature.
- If alternative data sources were not available, expert opinions were used, preferably from two or more experts. The experts were asked to score the specific subparameter from 1 (bad) to 5 (excellent). If needed, these scores were scaled to the required scale level of that subindicator.

The key dimension tables of AWDO 2016 (Appendixes 2–6) clearly specify (in bold and/or color) which data were "missing" and which approach was used to include a value for that specific subindicator. This methodology report contains some more background information on how this was done for the five key indicators.

3.4 Dealing with "Nonrelevant" Subindicators

Some subindicators appear to be not or hardly relevant in certain economies. Examples are storm surges or coastal flooding (key dimension 5) for landlocked countries such as Mongolia, Nepal, and Bhutan, or agriculture (key dimension 2) for city states like Singapore and Hong Kong, China. In those cases, we have dropped the nonrelevant subindicators and corrected the formulas used accordingly to make sure that the resulting (sub) indicators remain comparable.

A special category in this respect is the small island states for which the general methodology of AWDO was difficult to apply. How AWDO 2016 dealt with these small island states will be described in Appendix 2.

4 Key Dimension 1: Household Water Security

Key dimension 1 (KD1) provides an assessment of the extent to which countries are satisfying their household water and sanitation needs and improving hygiene for public health in all communities. The indicator describes the water, sanitation, and hygiene (WASH) component of water management.

Household water security is a composite of three subindicators:

- access to piped water supply (%);
- access to improved sanitation (%); and
- hygiene, quantified by disability-adjusted life years (DALYs) per 100,000 people for the incidence of diarrhea.

This indicator was originally developed for AWDO 2013 by the United Nations Economic and Social Commission for Asia and the Pacific (ESCAP). The application (and adjustments) for AWDO 2016 was performed by the Asia-Pacific Center for Water Security of Tsinghua University in Beijing, People's Republic of China. A detailed description of this application is given in APCWS (2015).

4.1 Assessment Framework

The assessment framework for key dimension 1 is illustrated in Figure 3.

All the three subindicators are scored between 1 and 5 against a set of predefined criteria based on their original data. The total KD1 score is the sum of these three subindicators.

This assessment framework is basically the same as the one used for AWDO 2013. A point to note for AWDO 2016 is that the method used by the World Health Organization (WHO) to estimate the diarrhea DALYs has been changed. How this is taken into account is described in section 4.3.3. For all three subindicators, the latest data have been used.

4.2 Subindicators: Access to Piped Water Supply and Access to Improved Sanitation

4.2.1 Data Source Used

Data on access to piped water supply for countries and territories in Asia and the Pacific for 2014 are based on the 2015 progress report on sanitation and drinking water published by WHO and UNICEF (JMP 2015). The data, also published online at http://www.wssinfo.org/data-estimates/tables, are considered to be the most authorized source for these indicators.

4.2.2 Scoring Table

The scoring criteria for access to piped water supply and improved sanitation are shown in Table 5. This is the same table as used for AWDO 2013.

It should be noted that this scoring is not linear. The table shows the lowest possible score of 1 is

Figure 3: Assessment Framework for Household Water Security (KD1)

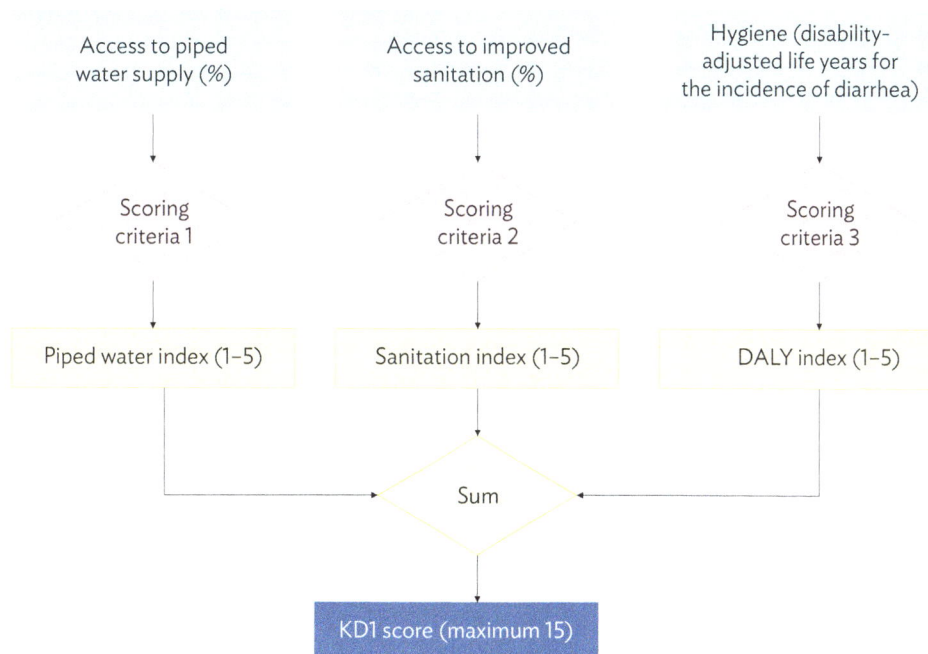

DALY = disability-adjusted life year, KD1 = key dimension 1.
Source: ADB.

Table 5: Scoring Table for Access to Piped Water Supply and Improved Sanitation

Access to Piped Water Supply and Improved Sanitation (%)	Score
<60	1
60–70	2
70–80	3
80–90	4
≥90	5

Source: ADB.

given if access is less than 60%. This may lead to some confusion, e.g., in cases where the percentage is about 50%, and readers might expect that this percentage of access to result in a score of 2 or 3.

A second remark to be made on this scoring table is that in certain cases it will not be possible (and necessary) to achieve the goal to have 100% access to piped water. Where piped water is economically not feasibly, other practical means of providing safe water to the people might be preferred. An example is the provision of water to migrating herders in Mongolia.

4.2.3 Changes from the Asian Water Development Outlook 2013

The data sources used for AWDO 2016 were the same as those used for AWDO 2013. Compared with AWDO 2013, there are some changes. For some countries (e.g., the Federated States of Micronesia and Nauru), access to piped water supply and improved sanitation were estimated based on expert judgment in AWDO 2013, but these data are now available for use in AWDO 2016. In analyzing the data used in AWDO 2013, we found some major discrepancies between the latest statistics and the expert estimates used in AWDO 2013. The access rate of piped water supply in the Federated States of Micronesia, for example, was estimated to be 94% in 2010 by experts for AWDO 2013. In the 2015 progress report on sanitation and drinking water, however, the country was reported to have a piped water access rate of only 37% in 2014. In Nauru, on the contrary, the access rate of piped water supply used in AWDO 2013 was judged to be 30% in 2010, while the 2015 progress report on sanitation and drinking water reported the data as 68% in 2014. A special case to mention is that Turkmenistan was found to have problems both of overestimation and underestimation. The expert estimates for access to piped water supply and improved sanitation in Turkmenistan were 72% and 62% in 2010 for AWDO 2013, respectively, while in the 2014 progress report on sanitation and drinking water, the data were 45% and 99%, respectively. Obviously, the inaccurate expert estimates of the missing data in AWDO 2013 confound the judgment on the progress made in improving

household water security in Asia and the Pacific between AWDO 2013 and AWDO 2016.

4.2.4 Missing Data

For both indicators, there are still countries and territories not included in the WHO/UNICEF database. These "missing" data are summarized in Table 6. For purposes of comparison, those areas with missing data in AWDO 2013 are also presented.

How Did We Deal with the Missing Data in the Asian Water Development Outlook 2016?

The missing data highlighted in Table 6 have been collected from additional data sources listed in Appendix 3 of the final report on KD1 (APCWS 2015). The quality of these estimates is considered to be high.

Table 6: Missing Data for Piped Water Supply and Access to Improved Sanitation in the Asian Water Development Outlook 2016 and 2013

Indicators	Missing Data in AWDO 2016	Missing Data in AWDO 2013
Access to piped water supply	Australia Brunei Darussalam Hong Kong, China Palau Republic of Korea Taipei,China Turkmenistan Uzbekistan	Australia Hong Kong, China Federated States of Micronesia Nauru Niue Taipei,China Tonga Turkmenistan
Access to improved sanitation	Brunei Darussalam Hong Kong, China New Zealand Taipei,China Turkmenistan Tuvalu	Hong Kong, China Taipei,China Turkmenistan

AWDO = Asian Water Development Outlook.
Source: ADB.

4.3 Subindicator: Hygiene

The subindicator for hygiene is quantified by the DALY index which stands for disability-adjusted life years per 100,000 people for the incidence of diarrhea.

4.3.1 Data Source Used

The basic source of data for DALY is provided by WHO. They publish their data online (at http://www.who.int/healthinfo/global_burden_disease/estimates/en/index1.html). The same source was used for AWDO 2013. One issue is that WHO has developed a simplified method for the estimation of DALYs wherein the age-weighting and time discounting is dropped (WHO 2013). This makes the DALY data before and after that adjustment no longer comparable. For AWDO 2016, we make use of the latest 2012 estimates for diarrhea DALYs. For AWDO 2013, the 2004 age-standardized estimates were used. By adjusting the scoring table (see section 4.3.2), the resulting subindicator scores have been made comparable.

4.3.2 Scoring Table

Due to changes in WHO's method for estimating the DALYs, the 2012 estimates of the diarrhea

Table 7: Scoring Criteria for Diarrhea Disability-Adjusted Life Years in the Asian Water Development Outlook 2016

Diarrhea DALYs per 100,000 people	Score
<190	5
190–500	4
500–1,200	3
1,200–1,800	2
≥1,800	1

Source: ADB.

DALYs used to represent the hygiene status in AWDO 2016 are not directly comparable with the 2004 estimates of age-standardized diarrhea DALYs used in AWDO 2013. Thus, it was necessary to adjust the scoring criteria used in AWDO 2013. The new scoring is given in Table 7. How this was done is described in the next section.

4.3.3 Changes from the Asian Water Development Outlook 2013

The change in WHO's method for estimating the DALYs made it necessary to adjust the scoring criteria of AWDO 2013. What made it difficult to rescale the scoring criteria is that the original method was applied to estimate the 2002 and 2004 DALYs, while the new one was used to get the 2000 and 2012 estimates instead. There is no year in which a DALY estimation using both methods are available. The diarrhea DALYs estimated with the new method decreased significantly in 32 out of 36 countries and territories in Asia and the Pacific from 2000 to 2012, whereas the age-standardized diarrhea DALYs estimated with the original method increased in 25 out of 46 from 2002 to 2004. The former suggests a decreasing trend of diarrhea DALYs in the long term in the Asia and Pacific region, while the latter likely indicates the interannual variability of diarrhea incidence, which may be more prominent during a short period of time than the impact of the long-term decreasing trend. Therefore, this study took advantage of the historical diarrhea DALYs, although estimated using two different methods, to rescale the scoring criteria for the new method. With the adjusted scoring criteria, the DALY index in 2000 for Asia and Pacific should be close to or a little lower than that in 2002 and in 2004, considering the short intervals among these 3 years, while the DALY index in 2012 should be higher than that in 2002 and in 2004. Based on these rules, the scoring criteria for diarrhea DALYs in AWDO 2016 could be derived and are shown in Table 7. A comparison of the DALY index in 2000, 2002, 2004, and 2012 for the Asia and Pacific region is described in the final report on KD1 (APCWS 2015).

A second change in the methodology of scoring KD1 between AWDO 2013 and AWDO 2016 is the way in which the overall score of KD1 is calculated. In AWDO 2013, the scores of the three subindicators were added together. This sum was then converted to a KD1 score between 1 and 5. In preparing AWDO 2016, it was discovered that the criteria used in the table for AWDO 2013 were very nonlinear, which resulted in lower bias KD1 results. After consultation of the experts involved in AWDO 2016, a correction was made in these criteria. The result is given in Table 8, which includes the old (2013) and new (2016) criteria.

This information is given for comparison purposes on KD1 between AWDO 2016 and AWDO 2013 only. As is explained in Chapter 9, we have decided to use a different approach for the scoring of the individual key dimensions and for the overall NWSI. In this new approach, only the sum of the subindicators is used. The conversion to an index between 1 and 5 is no longer done in determining the NWSI.

4.3.4 Missing Data

The countries/territories for which WMO does not provide data are summarized in Table 9. Those countries/territories with missing data in AWDO 2013 are also presented for a comparison purpose. For the hygiene indicator, as shown in the table, 10 countries/territories from the Pacific region lack estimated data for the year 2012 as compared with AWDO 2013.

4.4 How Did We Deal with the Missing Data in the Asian Water Development Outlook 2016?

The scores of the missing DALYs were determined based on expert judgment. See Appendix 2 on how this was done.

Table 8: Scoring Criteria for the Household Water Security (KD1) Index

Sum of Subindicators AWDO 2016	Sum of Subindicators AWDO 2013	Overall KD1 Score
<5	<4	1
5 to <8	4 to <7	2
8 to <11	7 to <13	3
11 to <14	13 to <14	4
≥14	≥14	5

AWDO = Asian Water Development Outlook, KD1 = key dimension 1.
Source: ADB.

Table 9: Missing Data for Disability-Adjusted Life Years in the Asian Water Development Outlook 2016 and 2013

Indicators	Missing Data in AWDO 2016	Missing Data in AWDO 2013
Diarrhea DALYs Access to improved sanitation	Cook Islands Hong Kong, China Kiribati Marshall Islands Federated States of Micronesia Nauru Palau Samoa Taipei,China Tonga Tuvalu	Hong Kong, China Taipei,China

AWDO = Asian Water Development Outlook.
Source: ADB.

4.5 Overall Assessment of Household Water Security in the Asian Water Development Outlook 2016

The determination of KD1 is the most straightforward of all the key dimensions. All three subindicators are intuitively the right ones and are being monitored by respected UN agencies. Although this key dimension has some data issues, most of these could be solved using other sources.

AWDO 2013 (and AWDO 2016) explicitly decided to use access to piped water supply on premises as its indicator for drinking water supply. The Joint Monitoring Programme also includes a category for safe water supply (e.g., by standpipes). Moreover, it was decided that access of less than 60% would result in a minimal score of 1. These are high standards that suppress the score for KD1 substantially. Local conditions (e.g., rural areas in Mongolia) might prevent certain countries from achieving higher scores.

An issue with the subindicators piped water supply and access to improved sanitation is that these indicators describe only the presence of the infrastructure and not the reliability and quality (e.g., of drinking water availability) of the services provided (see also the discussion in section 6 on urban water security about this reliability and quality issue).

5 Key Dimension 2: Economic Water Security

Key dimension 2 (KD2) describes the extent to which countries are able to satisfy the need of the economic sectors (food, industry, and energy) for water of sufficient quantity and quality. Economic water security is based on the performance of four subindicators—a general one and three specific sector subindicators:

- broad economy—describing the general water-related boundary conditions for the use of water for economic purposes,
- agriculture—indicating water productivity in agriculture and food security,
- energy—indicating water productivity in energy generation and energy security, and
- industry—indicating water productivity in industry.

The approach to KD2 in AWDO 2016 is significantly different from the approach followed in AWDO 2013. Still, the ultimate KD2 scores in AWDO 2016 are comparable to the scores presented in AWDO 2013. The KD2 approach has been developed by the International Water Management Institute (IWMI). A detailed description of the approach and application of KD2 for AWDO 2016 is given in IWMI (2015).

5.1 Assessment Framework

The assessment framework for KD2 is illustrated in Figure 4. The scores of the subindicators are determined by averaging the scores of their sub-subindicators. In one case (for the reliability sub-subindicator), further refinement was necessary

by taking into account three components. The scores of the sub-subindicators are determined by a scoring table that is explained later. The total KD2 score is the sum of these four subindicators.

This assessment framework has been changed considerably compared with the one that was used for AWDO 2013. The most important change is the addition of the broad economy subindicator. This subindicator measures the national conditions that are presumed to enable the contribution of water to the three economic sectors. These three economic sector subindicators are the same as in AWDO 2013 but are based now on a different set of sub-subindicators.

Data were utilized from a combination of recent sources. These are described by subindicator in the next sections. Data depth varies across sources (e.g., gross domestic product and population) and some across years (i.e., country's total dam capacity). Most data gaps were detected in the case of small island countries. To the extent possible, data were extrapolated to the year 2013.

5.2 Subindicator: Broad Economy

The degree to which basic elements are present to enable a functioning economy across sectors in a country was treated as a composite of four sub-subindicators: (i) reliability of supply across sectors, (ii) freshwater stress, (iii) the Storage–Drought Duration Index, and (iv) data availability. The first three sub-subindicators are focused on water availability for economic use, the last one on

Figure 4: Assessment Framework for Economic Water Security (KD2)

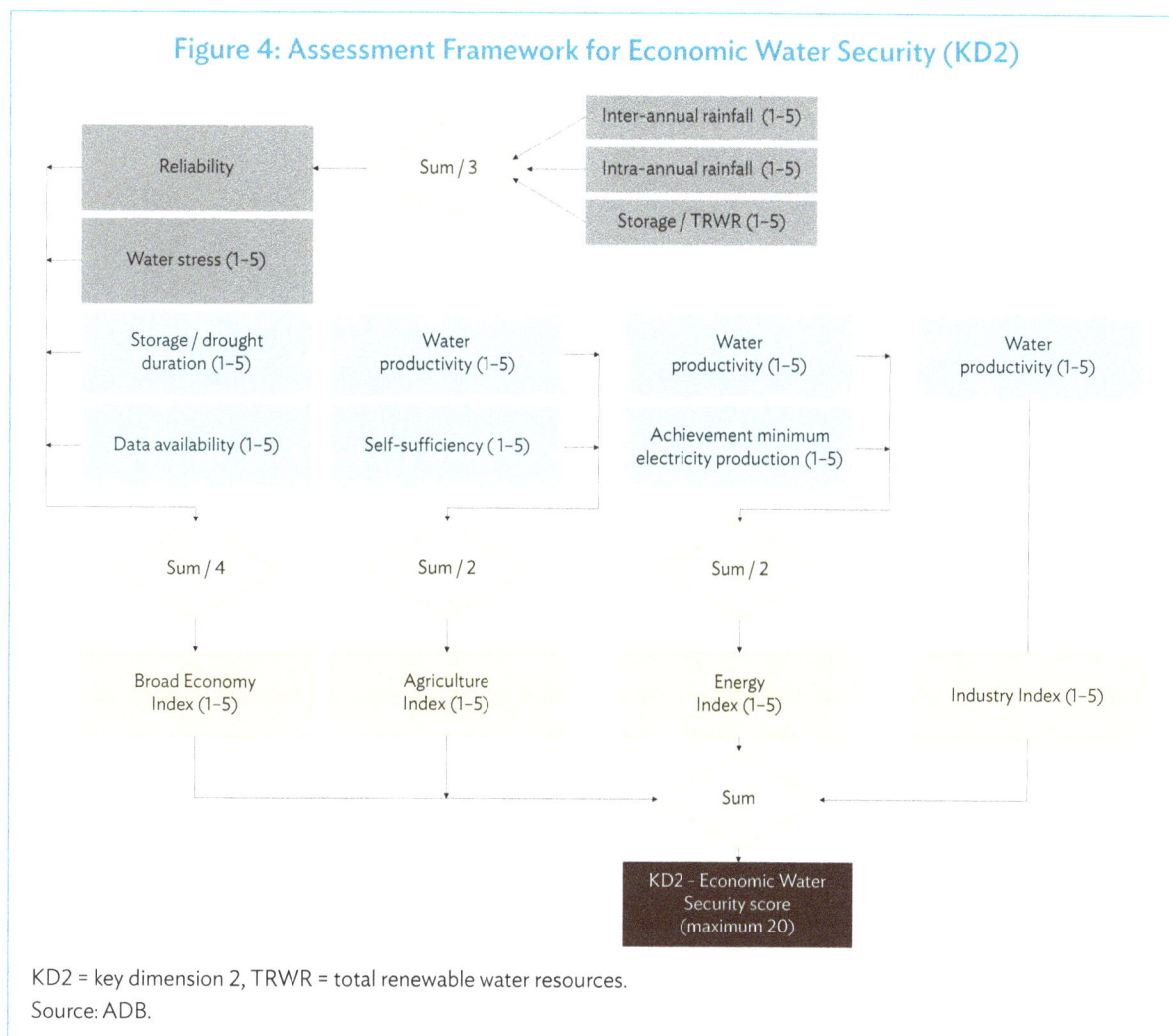

KD2 = key dimension 2, TRWR = total renewable water resources.
Source: ADB.

data availability for decision-making. The sub-subindicators and the logic behind them are listed in Table 10.

5.2.1 Data Sources Used

An overview of the data sources is given in Table 11.

Reliability. The degree to which countries have achieved assurance of stable supply across sectors was assessed by coupling results of two indicators: (i) rainfall coefficient of variation between and within years and (ii) storage divided by total renewable water resources. A lower rainfall coefficient of variation and higher ratio of storage

to total renewable water resources indicate that a country is more resilient to changes. Conversely, a higher rainfall coefficient of variation and lower ratio of storage to total renewable water resources indicate that a country is less prepared for water fluctuations. Data from Harris et al. (2014) on the monthly country-level precipitation for 1901–2013 and the FAO AQUASTAT (2015) data on the total country's dam capacity and the total renewable water resources were utilized. The data on total renewable water resources for each country remained constant across years (e.g., constant in 2002, 2007, 2012, and 2014). Thus, we used the 2014 data. The latest data on a country's dam capacity were somewhat variable but most often were from 2010. For AWDO 2016, we assumed

Table 10: Sub-subindicators of Broad Economy

Sub-subindicator	Indicator Logic	Measure
Assurance of stable supply across sectors	A country's economic activities are more assured when there is enough storage to assure reliable and timely supply and to mitigate risk.	Coefficient of variation of rainfall between and within years and storage/TRWR
Water stress	Water that is more stressed is less sustainable, more precarious, and a less secure input to economic activities.	Total freshwater withdrawal/TRWR
Storage–Drought Duration (Length) Index	Countries with a higher capacity to sustain droughts provide higher water security to economic activities.	(Total dam capacity/total freshwater withdrawal per month)/mean annual drought duration
Data availability	Lack of data obstructs assessment, monitoring, and decision-making, and is a threat to economic activities.	Availability of eight key data points were assessed: water storage, groundwater and surface freshwater withdrawals, industrial freshwater withdrawal, sector gross domestic product, water footprint, total electricity generation, electricity generation by source, and monthly country-level rainfall data

TRWR = total renewable water resources.
Source: ADB.

Table 11: Data Sources Used for Broad Economy

Sub-subindicator	Unit	Data Source
Assurance of stable supply across sectors/ reliability	%	Harris et al. (2014); FAO AQUASTAT (2015)
Water stress	%	World Bank (2015b); FAO AQUASTAT (2015)
Storage–Drought Duration (Length) Index	Fraction	Eriyagama, Smakthin, and Gamage (2009); New et al. (2002); FAO AQUASTAT (2015); World Bank (2015b)
Data availability	No. of data points	ADB (2015a, 2015b, 2015c); FAO AQUASTAT (2015); Harris et al. (2014); Hoekstra and Mekonnen (2012); IEA (2015); USEIA (n.d.); World Bank (2015b)

TRWR = total renewable water resources.
Source: ADB.

storage capacities to not have changed since the last year for which data were available.

Water stress. Total freshwater stress was measured as total annual freshwater withdrawal divided by total renewable water resources. A lower proportion of renewable water resources that are withdrawn indicates greater water security for economic growth and production. Data from the World Bank (2015b) on the total annual freshwater

withdrawals and the FAO AQUASTAT (2015) on total renewable water resources were utilized. The latest available data on the total annual freshwater withdrawals from 2013 were used in the calculations. The FAO AQUASTAT (2015) data on total renewable water resources for each country remained constant across years (e.g., constant in 2002, 2007, 2012, and 2014). Thus, we used the 2014 data.

Storage–Drought Duration Index. The assessment of countries' capacity to sustain droughts was conducted in two steps: (i) determining the number of months that a country's dam capacity is able to provide reliable water supply and (ii) dividing the number of months with reliable water supply by mean annual drought duration. A higher proportion of months with reliable water supply indicates greater water security for economic activities. This indicator was derived from Eriyagama, Smakthin, and Gamage (2009). Data from New et al. (2002) on mean annual drought duration were utilized. The latest available World Bank (2015b) data on the total annual freshwater withdrawals from 2013 were used in the calculations. Data on a country's total dam capacity was obtained from FAO AQUASTAT (2015).

Data availability. Data availability was measured by the degree to which data were available to populate the indicators applied in the economic water security assessment framework. Eight data points were considered central to calculations and their availability for each country was assessed: data on water storage (FAO AQUASTAT 2015), groundwater and surface freshwater withdrawals (FAO AQUASTAT 2015), industrial freshwater withdrawal (World Bank 2015b; FAO AQUASTAT 2015), sectoral GDP (ADB 2015a, 2015b, 2015c; World Bank 2015b; FAO AQUASTAT 2015), water footprint (Hoekstra and Mekonnen 2012),

electricity generation (IEA 2015; USEIA, n.d.; ADB 2015b), electricity generation by source (IEA 2015),[1] and monthly country-level rainfall data (Harris et al. 2014). Countries were ranked according to the number of data that could be obtained.

5.2.2 Scoring Table

The scores of the sub-subindicators were determined by applying the scoring in Table 12.

5.2.3 Changes from the Asian Water Development Outlook 2013

The additional broad economy component contains four indicators, one of which is fairly consistent with an indicator used in AWDO 2013 and three of which are new. Resilience, the first of the four indicators in the (broad) economy component, was utilized in AWDO 2013. In AWDO 2013, it was placed within the agriculture component even though the issues it captures are broader than agriculture. Water stress, the second of the four indicators in the (broad) economy category, was not utilized in the previous AWDO version. It is nonetheless a widely accepted indicator and likely to be used (among other indicators) to measure progress toward Sustainable Development Goal 6

Table 12: Scoring Table for Broad Economy Subindicator

| Score | Reliability | | | Water Stress | Storage–Drought Duration | Data Availability |
	Interannual Rainfall CV	Intra-annual Rainfall CV	Storage/ TRWR			
1	>0.15	>0.75	<3%	>80%	<0.5	4 or fewer data points
2	0.1–0.15	0.60–0.75	3%–5%	40%–80%	0.5–1	5 data points
3	0.05–0.1	0.4–0.6	5%–20%	20%–40%	1–3	6 data points
4	0.025–0.05	0.2–0.4	20%–50%	10%–20%	3–5	7 data points
5	<0.025	<0.2	>50%	<10%	>5	All 8 data points

CV = coefficient of variability, TRWR = total renewable water resources.
Source: ADB.

---

[1] Although USEIA (n.d.) and World Bank (2015b) contained relevant data, they lacked the degree of detail necessary for our calculations and were excluded from consideration.

of water and sanitation for all. The Storage–Drought Duration Index, which was not utilized in AWDO 2013, captures the ability of countries to satisfy their water demands in light of a typical annual drought. This indicator is viewed as a value addition in this AWDO update. The final indicator in the (broad) economy component is focused on data availability. It arose in response to feedback provided on previous versions of the AWDO 2016 economic water security framework. We believe this indicator to be a valuable addition.

5.2.4 Missing Data

All data for this subindicator were available and no action was needed.

5.3 Subindicator: Agriculture

The degree to which water is secured to enable agricultural production in a country was treated as a composite of two indicators: (i) water productivity in agriculture and (ii) self-sufficiency of agricultural production. The sub-subindicators and the logic behind them are listed in Table 13.

5.3.1 Data Sources Used

An overview of the data sources is given in Table 14.

Water productivity in agriculture. Water productivity in the agriculture sector was measured by agricultural gross domestic product (GDP) divided by a country's agricultural evapotranspiration (AgrET). Greater agricultural water productivity indicates higher water security. Data on the percentage of agricultural value-added to GDP and total GDP in 2013 were obtained from the World Bank (2015b).[2] To estimate AgrET at the country level, annual actual evapotranspiration data were obtained from the MODIS Global Evapotranspiration Project (MOD16) for 2013 and compared with actual evapotranspiration dataset for yearly actual evapotranspiration available on the FAO Geonetwork website (FAO, n.d.). Cultivated land area was then obtained from the Global Agro-Ecological Zones (GAEZ) for 2013 (IIASA and FAO, n.d.).[3] Finally, AgrET for cultivated land was clipped from the global evapotranspiration dataset using geographic information system (GIS). In GIS, the actual AgrET for every country was averaged to come up with the country AgrET in millimeters per year (mm/year). The volume of AgrET (in cubic kilometers, km^3) was determined by first converting

Table 13: Sub-subindicators of Agriculture

Sub-subindicator	Indicator Logic	Indicator Measure
Water productivity in agriculture	Productive agricultural water use allows the greatest production per unit of water use, thereby freeing up maximum water for other uses. Further, it is likely that more productive water use will enable coping with scarcity driven by population growth.	Total agricultural production/total agricultural water depletion
Self-sufficiency of agricultural production	Countries that satisfy a greater proportion of their agricultural good consumption from in-country sources are considered more secure and less vulnerable to global fluctuations in availability and price.	Ratio of agricultural goods consumption to agricultural good production, i.e., net virtual water imports in agriculture

Source: ADB.

---

[2]   For Myanmar and Taipei,China, the agricultural value-added to GDP and the total GDP data from ADB (2015c) were used. For the Marshall Islands and Samoa, the agricultural value-added to GDP data from ADB (2015c) were utilized. The agricultural value-added to GDP for eight countries (i.e., the Marshall Islands, the Federated States of Micronesia, Myanmar, New Zealand, Papua New Guinea, Solomon Islands, Timor-Leste, and Turkmenistan) was extrapolated to 2013 using linear trends. Total GDP for Myanmar was extrapolated to 2013 using linear trends.

[3]   Cultivated land area refers to both irrigated and rainfed areas.

Table 14: Data Sources Used for Agriculture

Sub-subindicator	Unit	Data Source
Water productivity in agriculture	$ million/ km³	IIASA and FAO (n.d.); MOD 16 (n.d.); World Bank (2015b)
Self-sufficiency of agricultural production	Fraction	ADB (2015a, 2015b, 2015c); Hoekstra and Mekonnen (2012); World Bank (2015b)

km³ = cubic kilometer.
Source: ADB.

the AgrET in millimeters per year to kilometers per year and multiplying by the cultivated land area (in square kilometers, km²). The estimated AgrET covers both rainfed and irrigated areas for the selected countries.[4]

Self-sufficiency of agricultural production. Sufficiency of agricultural production was measured as the annual water footprint of agricultural goods consumption divided by the annual water footprint of agricultural goods production. National-scale annual water footprint statistics data on agricultural goods consumption and agricultural goods production from Hoekstra and Mekonnen (2012) were used.[5] Both internal and external water footprints[6] were added to determine the country-level total water footprint of agricultural goods consumption and production. Given that the annual water footprint data from Hoekstra and Mekonnen (2012) reflected the situation up to 2005, their data were extrapolated to 2013 using secondary indicators. The annual water footprint data on agricultural goods consumption were extrapolated to 2013 based on population change. The country-level population data were obtained from ADB (2015a; 2015b; 2015c). The annual water footprint data on agricultural goods production

were extrapolated to 2013 by multiplying the 2005 country value by the ratio of the respective country's agricultural GDP change between 2005 and 2013. As mentioned earlier, the latest available agricultural value-added to GDP and total GDP data from 2013 were obtained from World Bank (2015b).[7]

5.3.2 Scoring Table

The scores of the sub-subindicators were determined by applying the scoring in Table 15.

Table 15: Scoring Table for Agriculture Subindicator

Score	Water Productivity in Agriculture ($ million/km³)	Self-Sufficiency of Agricultural Production
1	0–100	>3
2	100–200	1.5–3
3	200–350	1–1.5
4	350–1,000	0.5–1
5	>1,000	<0.5

km³ = cubic kilometer.
Source: ADB.

---

[4] The agricultural land area from FAO is smaller than the cultivated area data from GAEZ. The data from FAO is based on estimates, which could have given rise to the differences. Similarly with the evapotranspiration data, as the evapotranspiration data from FAO dataset are lower those from the MOD16 dataset. This difference could be a result of the FAO-56 equations used to derive the dataset. For that reason, the MOD16 datasets are preferred over the FAO estimates.

[5] Agricultural goods production excludes the water footprint of grazing and animal water supply.

[6] The internal footprint is the part of the water footprint of national consumption that falls inside the nation; the external footprint is the part outside the nation; see waterfootprint.org/en/waterfootprint/glossary for additional information.

[7] See footnote 3.

5.3.3 Changes from the Asian Water Development Outlook 2013

Indicators used in the agriculture component were consistent with those for AWDO 2013. The calculation of the agricultural water productivity indicator has nonetheless been refined. Agricultural evapotranspiration has now been calculated at the country level. This is presumed to reflect the water depleted to enable agricultural production. In AWDO 2013, a coarser method was utilized.

5.3.4 Missing Data

The data for the Cook Islands and Nauru were missing. It was decided that AWDO 2016 will not estimate the agricultural score of these countries. Instead, expert opinions on the overall score of KD2 were used (see section 5.6 for how this was done).

5.4 Subindicator: Energy (in Terms of Electricity)

The degree to which water security for the energy sector is achieved in a country was treated as a composite of two indicators: (i) water productivity in energy and (ii) achievement of a minimum platform for electricity production. The sub-subindicators and the logic behind them are listed in Table 16.

5.4.1 Data Sources Used

An overview of the data sources is given in Table 17.

Water productivity in energy. The water productivity of energy production was measured as electricity production (in gigawatt-hours, GWh)

Table 17: Data Sources Used for Energy

Sub-subindicator	Unit	Data
Water productivity in energy	GWh/km³	Gerbens-Leenes, Hoekstra, and Meer (2008); IPCC (2012); IEA (2015); Mekonnen, Gerbens-Leenes, and Hoekstra (2015)
Achievement of minimum platform for electricity production	kWh/cap	ADB (2015a; 2015b); USEIA (n.d.)

GWh = gigawatt-hour, km³ = cubic kilometer, kWh = kilowatt-hour.
Source: ADB.

Table 16: Sub-subindicators of Energy

Sub-subindicator	Indicator Logic	Indicator Measure
Water productivity in energy	Greater productivity indicates lower water requirements, and lower water requirements can be more easily satisfied and are therefore more secure.	energy production/water consumption A country's diversity of energy sources was linked to global consumption averages for those energy sources to determine water consumption associated with energy production
Achievement of minimum platform for electricity production	Countries with below-average per capita electricity production levels for Asia and the Pacific are presumed to be less water-secure as growth of energy production in future may require increased water withdrawal, thus creating stress on water storage and potential conflict with other water uses.	Present per capita electricity production and additional installed capacity needed to raise per capita power production to the per capita average in Asia and the Pacific

Source: ADB.

divided by the quantity of water consumed (in cubic kilometers, km^3) to produce that electricity. Electricity production data were obtained from IEA (2015), which contained the most detailed data from 2012 on country's electricity production from 13 sources:[8] coal, oil, gas, biofuels, waste, nuclear, hydro, geothermal, solar photovoltaic, solar thermal, wind, tide, and a category named "other sources." For consistency in calculations, the following five assumptions were made:

(i)   Consistent with the assumption of Mekonnen, Gerbens-Leenes, and Hoekstra (2015), water consumption of energy production from waste was considered 0.

(ii)   Median water consumption, rather than the lowest or the highest values, was used to calculate the water footprints of energy derived from coal, gas, nuclear, geothermal, solar photovoltaic, solar thermal, and wind sources.

(iii) Water consumption for energy generation from biofuels (described by the IEA only as the total of solid biofuels and biogas) was assumed to be equal to the water consumption for energy generation from biomass, and the water footprint for biomass-derived energy (average data from Brazil, the Netherlands, the United States, and Zimbabwe) was obtained from Gerbens-Leenes, and Hoekstra (2008).

(iv)   Water consumption for hydropower is affected by the reservoir design, climate, and allocation to other uses (IEA 2012). To obtain a more globally reflective average of water consumption of hydroelectricity, the median IPCC (2012) values were utilized in calculations.

(v)   Electricity generated from the unspecified "other sources" was removed from calculations, which may have affected the results for two countries with data in this category: the Republic of Korea and New Zealand.

Ultimately, countries' water productivity in energy generation was calculated by dividing the total electricity production by total water consumption in energy generation. Countries' total water consumption in energy generation was calculated by adding water consumed to produce electricity from each of the 12 sources. Higher values indicate that a country is using less water per unit of energy generation and is presumed to be more water-secure as it is using water efficiently.

Minimum platform for electricity production. The degree to which the minimum platform for electricity production is achieved was measured by subtracting a country's per capita energy production from average per capita energy production in the Asia and Pacific region. Population data for 2012 were obtained from ADB (2015a, 2015b) and coupled with the latest available 2012 data on electricity production from USEIA (n.d.).[9] The average per capita electricity production for Asia and the Pacific was used as the minimum platform and individual countries' per capita electricity production was compared with the regional average to determine the additional capacity needed to achieve the minimum platform of per capita electricity production. Higher values indicate that a country is less water-secure as growth of energy production in future may require increased water withdrawal, thus creating stress on water storage and potential conflict with other water uses.

---

8   Data were available for 30 countries. No data were available for Afghanistan, Bhutan, the Cook Islands, Fiji, Kiribati, the Lao People's Democratic Republic, the Maldives, the Marshall Islands, the Federated States of Micronesia, Nauru, Niue, Palau, Papua New Guinea, Samoa, Solomon Islands, Timor-Leste, Tonga, Tuvalu, and Vanuatu.

9   Electricity production data for Timor-Leste were obtained from ADB (2015a). No data were available for the Marshall Islands, the Federated States of Micronesia, Palau, and Tuvalu. These four countries and Niue (which was missing the population data) were excluded in calculating the regional average per capita electricity production.

5.4.2 Scoring Table

The scores of the sub-subindicators were determined by applying the scoring in Table 18.

Table 18: Scoring Table for Energy Subindicator

Score	Water Productivity in Energy (in terms of electricity) (GWh/km³)	Achievement of Minimum Platform for Electricity Production
1	<10,000	≥30%
2	10,000–25,000	within 30%
3	25,000–50,000	within 20%
4	50,000–100,000	within 10%
5	≥100,000	Regional average or above

GWh = gigawatt-hour, km³ = cubic kilometer.
Source: ADB.

5.4.3 Changes from the Asian Water Development Outlook 2013

The indicators for the energy component are new. The new indicators take a broader approach to water–energy issues that extend beyond the hydropower focus of AWDO 2013. They further reflect the addition and input of energy expertise in the team; no such energy expertise was included in the KD2 team for AWDO 2013.

5.4.4 Missing Data

Data on the Marshall Islands, the Federated States of Micronesia, Palau, and Tuvalu were missing. It was decided that AWDO 2016 will not make an estimate for the energy score of these countries. Instead, expert opinions on the overall score of KD2 were used (see section 5.6 for how this was done).

5.5 Subindicator: Industry

Water security for industry was measured by industrial water productivity. Although industrial freshwater withdrawals are much lower than the agricultural withdrawals, they are higher than the domestic withdrawals and are growing in many countries as the industry sector grows (WWAP 2014). The sub-subindicator and the logic behind it are listed in Table 19.

5.5.1 Data Source Used

An overview of the data source is given in Table 20.

Table 20: Data Sources used for Industry

Sub-subindicator	Unit	Data
Industrial water productivity	$ million/km³	World Bank (2015b)

km³ = cubic kilometer.
Source: ADB.

Table 19: Sub-subindicator of Industry

Sub-subindicator	Indicator Logic	Indicator Measure
Industrial water productivity	If productivity of water in industry is high, its water allocation is likely to be secure due to its importance to the economy. Further, greater industrial water productivity implies that industrial water use is efficient and less imposing on other water uses as less water is withdrawn for the sector.	Industrial GDP/ industrial withdrawal

GDP = gross domestic product.
Source: ADB.

Industrial water productivity. Industrial water productivity was measured as industrial GDP divided by industrial water withdrawal. The latest available industrial value-added to GDP, total GDP, industrial freshwater withdrawal (as % of total), and total annual freshwater withdrawal data were obtained from World Bank (2015b).[10] A higher proportion of GDP to industrial water withdrawal indicates that productivity of water in industry is high and the water allocation is likely to be secure due to its importance to the economy.

5.5.2 Scoring Table

The score of the sub-subindicator was determined by applying the scoring in Table 21.

Table 21: Scoring Table for Energy Subindicator

Score	Industrial Water Productivity ($ million/km^3)
1	<2,100
2	2,100–5,500
3	5,500–20,000
4	20,000–50,000
5	>50,000

km^3 = cubic kilometer.
Source: ADB.

5.5.3 Changes from the Asian Water Development Outlook 2013

The indicator in the Industry component is the same as the one utilized in AWDO 2013. One indicator utilized to measure industry in the context of AWDO 2013 was dropped to reflect the reality that it may be peripheral to industrial production.

5.5.4 Missing Data

Data for Hong Kong, China and Taipei,China were not available, as well for 12 small island states. It was decided that AWDO 2016 will not estimate the agricultural scores of these economies. Instead, expert opinions on the overall score of KD2 were used (see section 5.6 for how this was done).

5.6 Overall Missing Data for Economic Water Security

Data appeared to be missing for the agriculture (2 countries), industry (14 countries), and energy (4 countries) subindicators. Five countries had missing data for two subindicators (the small island states of the Cook Islands, the Marshall Islands, the Federated States of Micronesia, Nauru, Palau, and Tuvalu). The other countries were missing only data for one subindicator. The score of KD2 is determined by adding the scores of four subindicators. The following practical method was applied to deal with the missing data:

- In the case of countries with data missing for only one subindicator, AWDO 2016 ignored that subindicator. The sum of the remaining three subindicators was multiplied with a factor 4/3 to determine the score of KD2.
- In the case of countries with data missing for two subindicators, AWDO 2016 used expert opinion (EO) to make an expert estimate of the overall KD2 score. The two missing subindicators were given 25% of the expert estimate of the KD2 score. This method means that 50% of the AWDO 2016 KD2 score is based on data and 50%

---

[10] Total GDP and industrial value added to GDP for Myanmar and Taipei,China were obtained from the ADB (2015c). Industrial value added to GDP for the Marshall Islands, Papua New Guinea, and Samoa were obtained from the ADB (2015c). The industrial value added to GDP for six countries (i.e., the Marshall Islands, the Federated States of Micronesia, New Zealand, Samoa, Timor-Leste, and Turkmenistan) was extrapolated to 2013 using the linear extrapolation. Total GDP and the industrial value added to GDP for Myanmar was extrapolated to 2013 using the linear extrapolation.

on expert opinion. For the expert opinion, see Appendix 2. Specifically, the following scores were given to the missing data:

o   Cook Islands: EO-index 2, EO-score 8, score for each subindicator 2.
o   Marshall Islands: EO-index 1, EO-score 4, score for each subindicator 1.
o   Federated States of Micronesia: EO-index 3, EO-score 12, score for each subindicator 3.
o   Nauru: EO-index 2, EO-score 8, score for each subindicator 2.
o   Palau: EO-index 2, EO-score 8, score for each subindicator 2.
o   Tuvalu: EO-index 1, EO-score 4, score for each subindicator 1.

5.7 Overall Assessment of Economic Water Security

The new approach to determine KD2 is a major improvement compared with the approach followed in AWDO 2013. Attention should be paid to the following points for further improvement on the methodology for KD2:

- groundwater is not taken into account yet, mainly due to lack of reliable data on safe yields; and
- the hydrological data (broad economy) could be combined with the hydrological data of KD5 (in case risk is included in KD5).

In addition, three caveats emerge in relation to the methods and results:

- First, the first of the two indicators on energy is focused on electricity production rather than consumption. While most production is consumed within the country in which it is produced, four countries export significant amounts of hydropower to its neighbors: Bhutan to India, the Lao People's Democratic Republic to Thailand, and the Kyrgyz Republic and Tajikistan to Uzbekistan and southern Kazakhstan. As such, electricity production per unit of water consumption reflects a higher quantity of water use than that needed to satisfy the domestic electricity consumption.
- Second, coastal and island countries may require less freshwater for cooling (for fossil fuel- and nuclear-based electricity production) as saltwater would be readily available. Possible stratification of countries into coastal and landlocked may strengthen the results. Nonetheless, it seems that nearly all states in Asia and the Pacific are islands or possess coasts.
- Third, industry results in certain countries (e.g., Cambodia, Nepal, and Timor-Leste) may be affected by their extremely small manufacturing base, which may have elevated their scores.

6 Key Dimension 3: Urban Water Security

Key dimension 3 (KD3) describes the progress the countries are making to provide better urban water services and management in order to develop vibrant, livable cities and towns. The concept behind KD3 in AWDO is based on the Water Sensitive Cities Framework of Brown, Keath, and Wong (2009) which is illustrated in Figure 5.

The urban water security indicator is based on the performance of the first four stages (drivers) in the Water Sensitive Cities Framework and is expressed by the following subindicators (see Table 22):

- piped urban water supply access (% of population),
- urban wastewater collected (% of population),
- economic damage due to floods and storms (% of GDP), and
- river health (taken from KD4).

The framing of urban water security in KD3 focuses predominantly on the state of water infrastructure assets and development within the first three stages. In doing so, it aims to assess the conditions of that infrastructure.

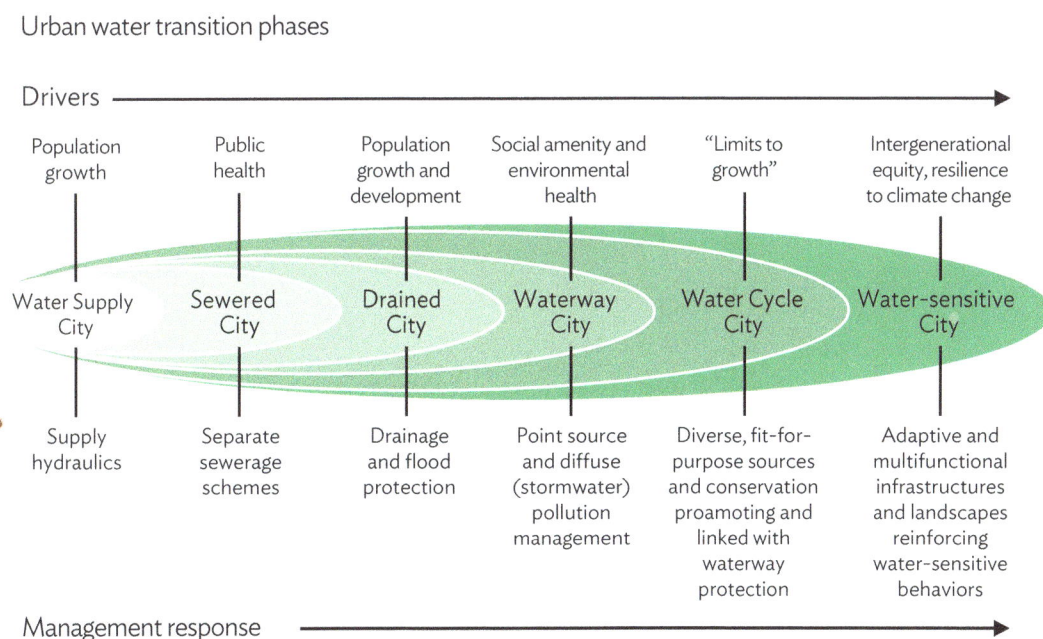

Figure 5: Water-Sensitive Cities Framework

Source: R. Brown, N. Keath, and T. Wong. 2009. Urban Water Management in Cities: Historical, Current, and Future Regimes. *Water Science and Technology* 59(5): 847–855.

Table 22: Summary of Subindicators for Urban Water Security

Subindicator	Indicator Logic	Indicator Measure
Wastewater index (sewered city)	The environment within and downstream of a city is more likely protected (including local groundwater quality) when wastewater is collected and treated effectively.	Urban wastewater collected (% of population)
Drainage index (drained city)	A city's water supply is more secure when there is less damage due to flooding and storms (i.e., due to extensive drainage infrastructure).	Economic damage due to floods and storms (% of GDP)
River health	Water security must be considered in the context of the management of the river basin or basins in which the city is located.	KD4 river health index (dimensionless 0–1)

GDP = gross domestic product, KD4 = key dimension 4.
Source: ADB.

To compare countries using the urban water security index, the following assumptions were made:

- Scores (1 lowest to 5 highest) for water supply, wastewater collection, and drainage infrastructure were used to compare countries, rather than absolute numbers. This nonparametric approach was used to reduce any error that may be associated with the assumptions and extrapolation processes in the development of derived data. This was required due to the limited availability of empirical data for the urban water security indicators.
- A waterway health factor (0 for average to poor, 1 for good to excellent) was derived from the KD4 river health index. This was used to assess the potential for urban areas to progress toward "water-sensitive cities."

A summary of the urban water security index indicators and the logic behind their development is contained in Table 23.

The approach to KD3 in AWDO 2016 is more or less the same as that followed in AWDO 2013. The KD3 approach has been developed by the International Water Center (IWC) in Australia. A detailed description of the KD3 methodology is given in IWC (2015a).

Table 23: Summary of Logic for Normalization for Urban Water Security Index

Normalization	Normalization Data	Normalization Logic
Urban growth	Urban growth rate (% population growth)	The urbanization rate reflects challenges to water security faced by rapidly expanding cities.

Source: ADB.

6.1 Assessment Framework

The assessment framework for KD3 is illustrated in Figure 6.

The first three subindicators are scored between 1 and 5 against a set of predefined criteria based on their original data. The fourth subindicator (river health) is taken from KD4 and was added to include water quality. To avoid excessive double-counting in the overall water security subindicator, a maximum value of 1 is given. Actually, only a value of 0 (poor to average) or 1 (good to excellent) is given. The urban growth rate was added to reflect the challenges to water security faced by rapidly expanding cities. A fast-growing city is given a low urban factor (0.8), while a stable city is given a

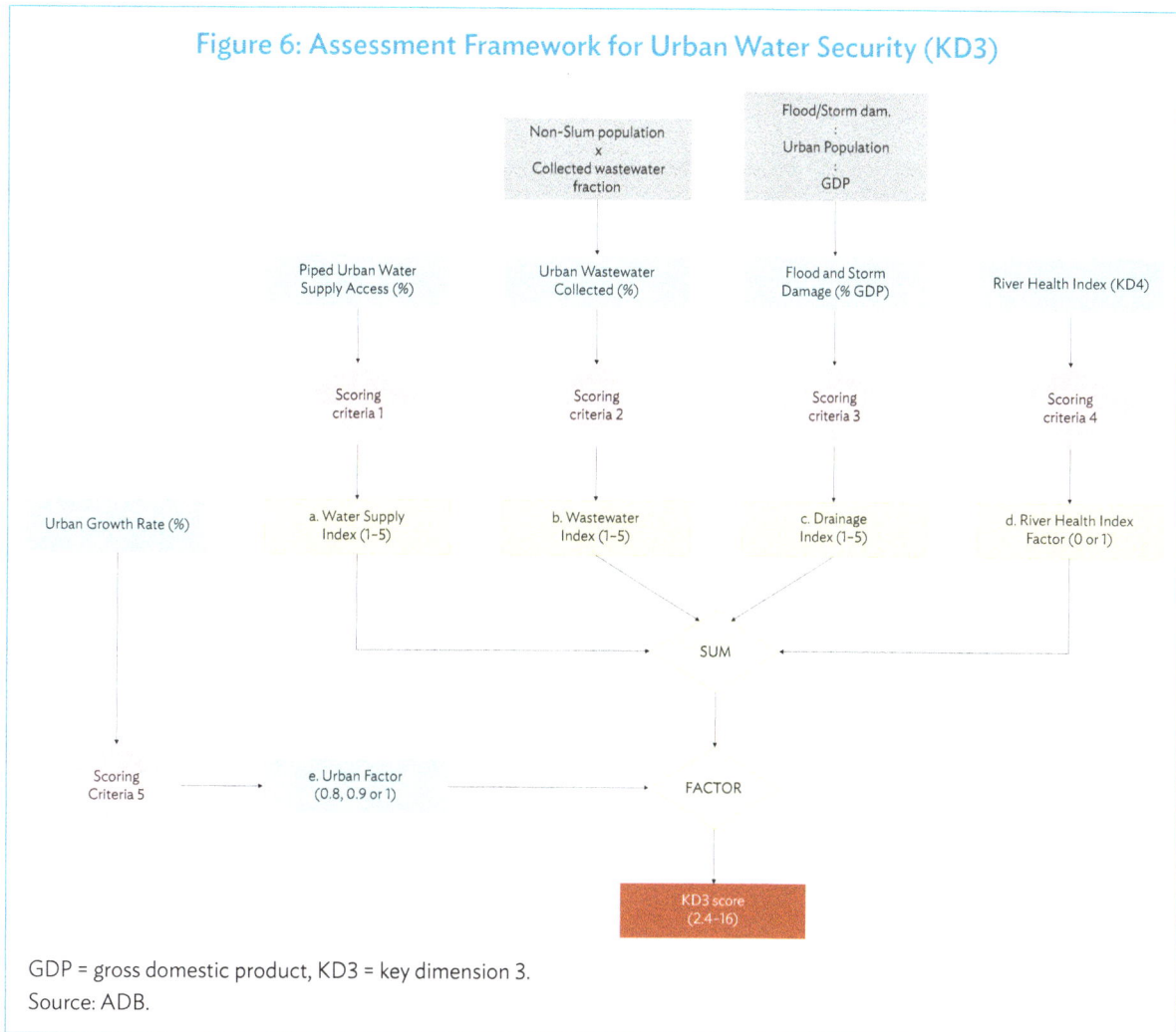

Figure 6: Assessment Framework for Urban Water Security (KD3)

GDP = gross domestic product, KD3 = key dimension 3.
Source: ADB.

factor of 1. The urban water security indicator is calculated by the formula $(a + b + c + d) \times e$.

This assessment framework is nearly exactly the same as the one used for AWDO 2013. The main changes are the maximum score for river health (which in AWDO 2013 was still 5) and the simplification of the calculation of the wastewater subindicator. This last change is described in Appendix 3 of the final report on KD3 (IWC 2015a).

6.2 Subindicator: Piped Urban Water Supply

6.2.1 Data Sources Used

The indicator for the water supply index was developed from urban piped water supply at the country level. The data were sourced from the WHO/UNICEF Joint Monitoring Programme (JMP) datasets for water supply and sanitation (JMP 2015) under the Millennium Development Goals program. This is considered only a surrogate indicator for water supply as it does not consider factors such as water source availability, quality of water supplied, pricing, and equity issues.

The current water supply indicator also does not consider water quality, pricing, and equity issues, or the variation in availability of the water service available to urban areas. In larger Asian cities, for example, more than one in five water supplies fail to meet the national water quality standards (WHO and UNICEF 2000). In addition, potable water services are not maintained full-time (24 hours per day, 7 days per week) at the point of delivery. For example, some cities in the People's Republic of China provide round-the-clock domestic water service, whereas that for Bangalore in India is not maintained full-time and water is only available from the tap for an average of 4 hours a day (Mahindru 2004).

It should be pointed out that where data for 2014 for piped water supply (%) were not available for a particular country, the most recently available data were used. This source was considered the best available data on water supply and sanitation access available. This is noted as comments in the calculation spreadsheet for the affected cells.

6.2.2 Scoring Table

The classification bands used for the urban water supply indicator are the same as in AWDO 2013. The classification bands for the water supply subindicator are outlined in Table 24.

Table 24: Classification Bands for the Water Supply Indicator (Scoring Criteria 1)

Water Supply Indicator	Water Supply (%)	Achievement of Minimum Platform for Electricity Production
1	0 to <60	60
2	60 to <70	10
3	70 to <80	10
4	80 to <90	10
5	90 to <100	10

Source: ADB.

6.3 Subindicator: Urban Wastewater Collected

6.3.1 Data Sources Used

The indicator for the wastewater index is the percentage of the population that has access to a sewage collection network at the country level. Empirical data were available for some countries and used in preference over derived data for this indicator. These empirical data were directly available from the Global Water Intelligence (GWI) water market report, such as for Australia, the People's Republic of China, and India (GWI 2014).

For countries for which empirical data were not readily available, the indicator was derived using the methodology outlined in Figure 7. The derived method used access to improved sanitation as a surrogate indicator for the proportion of wastewater that is collected (by population). The data for access to improved sanitation was taken from JMP (2015). The percentage of the population with wastewater collection facilities was then derived by correcting the access to improved sanitation (%) by the nonslum proportion of the population, sourced from the UN Millennium Development Goals database (UN 2015) (see Figure 7). This correction was performed to ensure that the wastewater collection percentage was representative of the entire population of an urban area, including both slum and nonslum areas (see details in Figure 8).

Wastewater collected (%) = Nonslum population (%) × Access to improved sanitation (%)

A conceptual flow diagram for this calculation is outlined in Figure 8.

6.3.2 Assumptions

The major assumption made in the development of the wastewater management subindicator is that the slum population does not have access

---

Figure 7: Methodology for the Sewered City Indicator for the Asian Water Development Outlook 2016

Non-Slum population
(Fraction of urban population)

UN-HABITAT, 2015

x

Collected wastewater fraction
(Access to improved sanitation [% of population])

Joint Monitoring Program, 2015

=

Wastewater Collected

Collected wastewater volume from slum to non-slum areas

Source: ADB.

Figure 8: Flow Diagram for the Sewered City Indicator for the Asian Water Development Outlook 2016

Urban non-slum areas

Wastewater Collected
(Population with access to improved sanitation)

Wastewater collection network

Wastewater Not Collected
(Population without access to improved sanitation)

Urban slum areas

Wastewater Not Collected (Slum Population)

Environment

Source: ADB.

---

to the city's wastewater collection and treatment network. A slum household is defined as a group of individuals living under the same roof and facing one or more of the following conditions: insecure residential status, inadequate access to safe water, inadequate access to sanitation, poor structural quality of housing, and overcrowding. As people living in urban slums or informal settlements frequently lack access to adequate water and sanitation, it is likely that the coverage in slum areas is much lower than the average for urban areas. The methodology assumes that the entirety of the slum population of a city is not connected to an improved sanitation source (e.g., flush or pour-flush to piped sewer system, septic tanks, pit latrines, or composting toilets) and therefore wastewater is unable to be collected or treated. This assumption was made as in the JMP data; urban figures are national averages and therefore may not reflect the situation in all urban areas such as slums. It has been noted in the previous literature that current national data collection and reporting to JMP often exclude slums and informal areas (ISF 2014, Musinguzi 2015).

Figure 9: Interpretation of Water Supply and Sanitation Data from the Joint Monitoring Programme

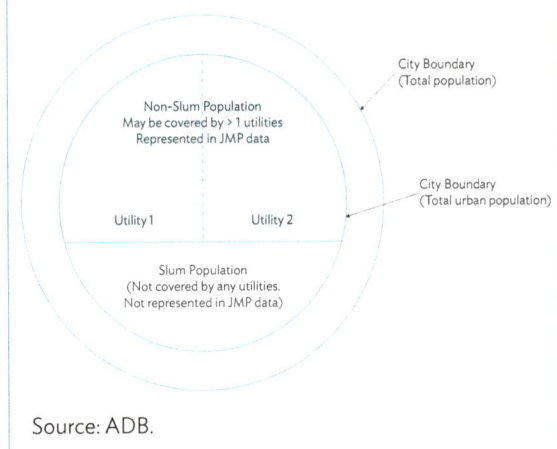

Source: ADB.

The interpretation of the JMP data used for the development of KD3 is outlined in Figure 9.

The methodology for this indicator incorporates this major assumption by adjusting the JMP's improved sanitation access (%) by a factor (i.e., nonslum percentage of the urban population). The derived value is expected to be more representative of the entire city population, not just the nonslum areas.

Other data collection assumptions include that the data for the percentage of population living in slum areas were mostly absent for the required data year. Where data for a country were available for years other than 2012, the data for 2012 were estimated based on linear interpolation (if data for multiple years were available) or the most recent data were used (if data were only available for a single year). Where slum fraction data for a country were unavailable, the regional average was used as a placeholder (e.g., South Asia for Bangladesh).

Data taken from the ESCAP and World Bank online databases are used without consideration to the assumptions and limitations in the original data collection, as listed in the footnotes in the raw data files.

6.3.3 Scoring Table

The classification bands used for the wastewater treatment subindicator are the same as for AWDO 2013 and are outlined in Table 25.

Table 25: Classification Bands for the Drainage Indicator (Scoring Criteria 2)

Wastewater Treatment Indicator	Wastewater Treatment (%)	Indicator Bandwidth
1	0 to <60	60
2	60 to <70	10
3	70 to <80	10
4	80 to <90	10
5	90 to <100	10

Source: ADB.

6.4 Subindicator: Flood and Storm Damage

6.4.1 Data Sources Used and Calculation Approach

The indicator for the drainage index was developed from the extent of economic damage as a result of flood and storm incidents in a country (i.e., economic damage per capita), compared against the vulnerability of its urban population against such incidents (i.e., GDP per capita). The methodology is summarized in Figure 10. This indicator was only available at the country level and datasets were sourced from the International Disaster Database for 2000–2014 (EM-DAT 2015). It serves as a surrogate for the extent of drainage infrastructure and flood protection in a country.

6.4.2 Scoring Table

The classification bands used for the drainage and flood protection indicator are the same as for AWDO 2013. The classification bands for the drainage subindicator are outlined in Table 26.

Figure 10: Methodology for the Drained City Indicator

Flood and Storm Damage
(Economic damage due to floods and storms, $)
International Disaster Database, 2000–2014

÷

Urban Population
(Total population x urbanization factor)
Joint Monitoring Program, 2015

÷

Gross Domestic Product
($ per capita)
World Bank, 2015

Index for Stormwater Drainage = GDP Standardized Damage

GDP = gross domestic product.
Source: ADB.

Table 26: Classification Bands for Drainage Indicator (Scoring Criteria 3)

Drainage Indicator	Standardized Flood Damage Loss, 2000–2014 (% of GDP)
5	0
4	0.5
3	6
2	10
1	14

GDP = gross domestic product.
Source: ADB.

6.5 River Health Correction Factor

A correction factor was included in the development of the overall urban water security index to account for a city's urban river management. This correction factor was applied based on the logic that a city's water security is higher if its near river basins are well-maintained and vice versa. The logic for the correction factor was developed based on personal communication with Eva Abal of IWC and follows the methodology used in AWDO 2013.

The national river basin health index from KD4 was used as a proxy indicator for urban river

management. The urban river management factor was assessed as 0 for a river basin health index value less than 3 and as 1 for an index value for 3 and above. The classification bands for the river health correction factor are outlined in Table 27.

Table 27: Classification Bands for River Health Factor (Scoring Criteria 4)

KD4 River Health Index	River Health Index Factor
5	1
4	1
3	1
2	0
1	0

KD4 = key dimension 4.
Source: ADB.

6.6 Urban Factor

A correction factor was included in the development of the overall urban water security index to account for a country's urbanization rate. This correction factor was applied based on the logic that a city's water security is higher if there is a lower rate of urbanization as investment in water, wastewater, and drainage infrastructure is more likely to match the rate of population growth and vice versa. The logic for the correction factor was developed based on personal communication with Eva Abal of IWC and follows the methodology used in AWDO 2013.

The urbanization rate was used to develop the urban factor. Data for the urbanization rate was sourced from ESCAP statistical databases (ESCAP 2015). The classification bands for the urban correction factor are outlined in Table 28.

6.7 Overview of Data Used and Missing Data

A summary of the data sources used for the KD3 analysis is contained in Table 29.

A summary of all data sources used by economy is contained in Table 30.

Table 28: Urban Correction Factor (Scoring Criteria 5)

Urbanization Rate (% per year)	Urbanization Correction Factor
< 2	1
2–3	0.9
> 3	0.8

Source: ADB.

Table 29: Summary of Data Sources for Urban Water Security for the Asian Water Development Outlook 2016

Index	Data	Source	Data Year
Water supply index	Urban piped water supply (%)	JMP (2015)	2014[a]
	Empirical data – wastewater collected (%)	GWI (2014)	2014
Wastewater index	Derived data – a. Slum population (% of urban population)	UN (2015)	2014[b]
	Derived data – b. Access to improved sanitation (% of population)	JMP (2015)	2014[a]
	A. Monetary damage due to flood and storms ($)	EM-DAT (2015)	2000–2014[c]
Drainage index	B. Urban population	JMP (2015)	
	C. GDP per capita ($/capita)	World Bank (2015a)[d] ESCAP (2015)	2014
Urban factor	Urban growth rate (% per year)	ESCAP (2015)	2014
River health index factor	River health index (KD4)	AWDO 2016	2015

GDP = gross domestic product, KD4 = key dimension 4.

Notes:

[a] Where data for 2014 for piped water supply (%) or access to improved sanitation (%) were not available for a particular country, the most recently available data were used. This source was considered the best available data on water supply and sanitation access available. This is noted as comments in the calculation spreadsheet for the affected cells.

[b] Where data for 2014 for the slum population were not available for a particular country, the most recently available data were used. Where no data were available for a particular country, data for the slum population for the region were used from the same source. This source was considered the best available data on slum population available. This is noted as comments in the calculation spreadsheet for the affected cells.

[c] No data were available in EM-DAT for Taipei city of Taipei,China. Data for Taipei,China were assumed to be a reasonable placeholder as no better data were available.

[d] Where data for 2014 for GDP per capita were not available for a particular country from the World Bank, data from ESCAP were used as it had data available for countries not identified by the World Bank. This is noted as comments in the calculation spreadsheet for the affected cells.

Source: ADB.

Table 30: Summary of Data Sources Used for Urban Water Security

Data Source	Water Supply	Wastewater Index			Drainage Index				Urban Factor	River Health Factor
	Piped Urban Water Supply Access (%) (JMP, 2015)	Empirical Wastewater Collected (%) (GWI, 2014)	Derived Data – Slum Population (% of Urban) (UN, 2015)	Derived Data – Access to Improved Sanitation (%) (JMP, 2015)	Monetary Damage – Flood and Storm (USD) (EMDAT, 2015)	Urban Population (JMP, 2015)	GP Data ($/capita) (World Bank, 2015)	GP Data ($/capita) (UNESCAP, 2015)	Urban Growth Rate (% per year) (UNESCAP, 2015)	KDA Rivver Health Index
Source Number	1	2	3	4	5	6	7		8	9
Afghanistan	✓		✓	✓	✓	✓	✓		✓	✓
Armenia	✓		✓	✓	✓	✓	✓		✓	✓
Australia	E	✓	✓	✓	✓	✓	✓		✓	✓
Azerbaijan	✓		✓	✓	✓	✓	✓		✓	✓
Bangladesh	✓		✓	✓	✓	✓	✓		✓	✓
Bhutan	✓		✓	✓	✓	✓	✓		✓	✓
Brunei Darussalam	✓		✓	A	✓	✓	✓		✓	✓
Cambodia	✓		✓	✓	✓	✓	✓		✓	✓
China, People's Republic of	✓	✓	✓	✓	✓	✓	✓		✓	✓
Cook Islands	✓		✓	✓	✓	✓		✓	✓	✓
Fiji	✓		✓	✓	✓	✓	✓		✓	✓
Georgia	✓		✓	✓	✓	✓	✓		✓	✓
Hong Kong, China	A		✓	A	✓	✓	✓		✓	✓
India	✓	✓	✓	✓	✓	✓	✓		✓	✓
Indonesia	✓	✓	✓	✓	✓	✓	✓		✓	✓
Japan	✓	✓	✓	✓	✓	✓	✓		✓	✓
Kazakhstan	✓		✓	✓	✓	✓	✓		✓	✓
Kiribati	✓		✓	✓	✓	✓	✓		✓	✓
Korea, Republic of	✓		✓	✓	✓	✓	✓		✓	✓
Kyrgyz Republic	✓		✓	✓	✓	✓	✓		✓	✓
Lao People's Democratic Republic	✓		✓	✓	✓	✓	✓		✓	✓
Malaysia	✓		✓	✓	✓	✓	✓		✓	✓
Maldives	✓		✓	✓	✓	✓	✓		✓	✓
Marshall Islands	✓		✓	✓	✓	✓		✓	✓	✓
Micronesia, Federated States of	✓		✓	✓	✓	✓	✓		✓	✓
Mongolia	✓		✓	✓	✓	✓	✓		✓	✓
Myanmar	✓		✓	✓	✓	✓	✓		✓	✓

continued on next page

Table 30 *continued*

Data Source	Water Supply	Wastewater Index			Drainage Index				Urban Factor	River Health Factor
	Piped Urban Water Supply Access (%) (JMP, 2015)	Empirical Wastewater Collected (%) (GWI, 2014)	Derived Data – Slum Population (% of Urban) (UN, 2015)	Derived Data – Access to Improved Sanitation (%) (JMP, 2015)	Monetary Damage – Flood and Storm (USD) (EMDAT, 2015)	Urban Population (JMP, 2015)	GP Data ($/capita) (World Bank, 2015)	GP Data ($/capita) (UNESCAP, 2015)	Urban Growth Rate (% per year) (UNESCAP, 2015)	KDA Rivver Health Index
Source Number	1	2	3	4	5	6	7		8	9
Nauru	✓		✓	✓	E	✓	✓	✓	✓	✓
Nepal	✓		✓	✓	✓	✓	✓		✓	✓
New Zealand	✓		✓	A	✓	✓	✓		✓	✓
Niue	✓		✓	✓	✓	✓	✓		✓	✓
Pakistan	✓		✓	✓	✓	✓	✓		✓	✓
Palau	✓		✓	✓	✓	✓	✓		✓	✓
Papua New Guinea	✓		✓	✓	✓	✓	✓		✓	✓
Philippines	✓	✓	✓	✓	✓	✓	✓		✓	✓
Samoa	✓		✓	✓	✓	✓	✓		✓	✓
Singapore	✓	✓	✓	✓	✓	✓	✓		✓	✓
Solomon Islands	✓		✓	✓	✓	✓	✓		✓	✓
Sri Lanka	✓		✓	✓	✓	✓	✓		✓	✓
Taipei,China	A		✓	A	E	✓	✓	✓	✓	✓
Tajikistan	✓		✓	✓	✓	✓	✓		✓	✓
Thailand	✓		✓	✓	✓	✓	✓		✓	✓
Timor-Leste	✓		✓	✓	✓	✓	✓		✓	✓
Tonga	✓		✓	✓	✓	✓	✓		✓	✓
Turkmenistan	✓		✓	O	✓	✓	✓		✓	✓
Tuvalu	✓		✓	✓	✓	✓	✓		✓	✓
Uzbekistan	✓		✓	✓	✓	✓	✓		✓	✓
Vanuatu	✓		✓	✓	✓	✓	✓		✓	✓
Viet Nam	✓	✓	✓	✓	✓	✓	✓		✓	✓

✓ = data available for 2014, [Blank] = no data available, A = data from Asian Water Development Outlook 2013, E = expert opinion applied, O = data for year other than 2014 available only.

Source: ADB.

6.8 Overall Assessment of Urban Water Security in the Asian Water Development Outlook 2016

KD3 addresses the specific water resource issues in cities. AWDO has decided to create KD3 as a separate key dimension given the growing importance of urban centers in Asia. It should be noted that the subindicators defined for KD3 are also included in other key dimensions:

- water supply – in KD1
- waste water – in KD1 and KD4
- drainage – in KD5

Using KD3 as a separate key dimension has a value on its own. Combining KD3 with the other key dimensions in an overall NWSI means that some double-counting takes place. The influence of this double-counting is analyzed in Appendix 4. The conclusion of this appendix is that the double-counting plays a certain role but that the main messages of AWDO 2016 on national water security

do not change. The logical conclusion is that countries with low KD3 scores will have somewhat higher NWS scores if KD3 is dropped and countries with high KD3 scores will have somewhat lower NWS scores.

The applied conceptual framework of KD3 is solid. However, further improvement is possible and desired given the improvement in available data and analysis concepts. The following are the recommendations for improvement:

- wider consideration of risk and opportunity (making the approach forward-looking),
- system for data compilation and analysis (in particular improving the IBNET database),
- water supply index assessment (using volumetric consumption and/or water mass balance analysis),
- wastewater index (volumetric and treatment),
- taking into account virtual water flows in water stress conditions, and
- data availability and consistency (e.g., what is urban).

Refer to the IWC (2015a) report for more details.

7 Key Dimension 4: Environmental Water Security

Key dimension 4 (KD4) describes how well a country is able to develop and manage its river basins with the aim of sustaining the ecosystem services the rivers provide.

The refined indicator for environmental water security comprises three separate components—the first being the sole indicator for KD4 in AWDO 2013, the river health index (RHI), and two new additional indicators:

(i)   river health index;
(ii) hydrologic alteration; and
(iii) governance of the environment.

Each of these represents a separate process that contributes to or reduces environmental water security. These indicators are combined in a simple mathematical framework to deliver a transparent picture of the state of environmental water security at the country level across the region. Combining the three indicators into a single index for KD4 provides a more complete picture of environmental water security than was used in AWDO 2013. The addition of subindicators for flow alteration and governance of the environment makes the ultimate KD4 result not directly comparable with the scores presented in AWDO 2013. A second change in the approach to KD4 is the development of a simpler model to determine the river health. This is explained in section 7.2.3.

The KD4 approach has been developed by the International Water Center (IWC) in Australia. A detailed description of the KD4 methodology is given in IWC (2015b).

7.1 Assessment Framework

The general assessment framework for KD4 is illustrated in Figure 11.

All the three subindicators are scored between 1 and 5. How this is done is explained in the next sections. The total KD4 score is the sum of these three subindicator scores.

The assessment framework is significant different than the one used for AWDO 2013.

7.2 Subindicator: River Health Index

The determination of the river health subindicator is fundamentally different from the other indicators as its value is determined based on a modeling exercise. The use of a model makes it possible to project future situations. This possibility has not been used for AWDO 2016. The RHI is determined on a pixel-based map and aggregated up to the country level. The driving forces for the RHI are (i) climate (changes in river flows), (ii) population growth, (iii) water demand, (iv) economic development (GDP), and (v) agricultural land use and production change. The statistical model was calibrated based on AWDO 2013 to ensure consistency between the AWDO results. The AWDO 2016 is based on 2010 data, while AWDO 2013 is based on 2000 data. The calculation approach is illustrated in Figure 12.

Figure 11: Assessment Framework for Environmental Water Security (KD4)

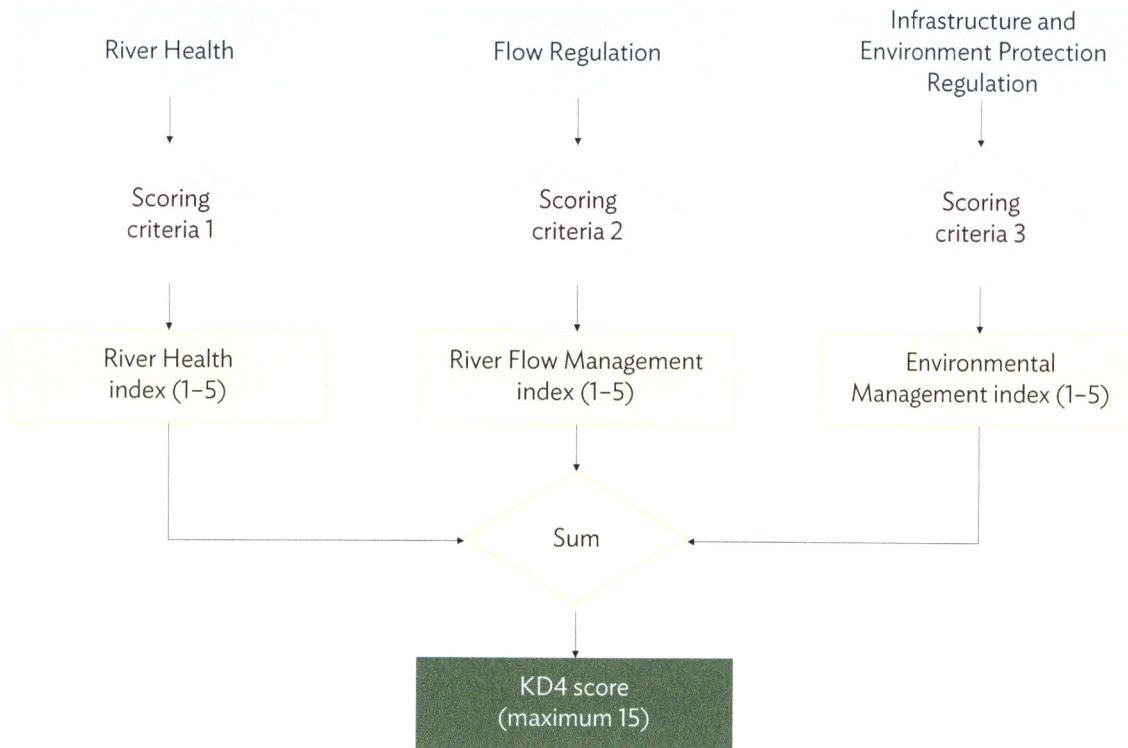

River Health   Flow Regulation   Infrastructure and Environment Protection Regulation

↓   ↓   ↓

Scoring criteria 1   Scoring criteria 2   Scoring criteria 3

↓   ↓   ↓

River Health index (1–5)   River Flow Management index (1–5)   Environmental Management index (1–5)

→   Sum   ←

↓

KD4 score (maximum 15)

KD4 = key dimension 4.
Source: ADB.

Figure 12: Calculation Approach for the River Health Index

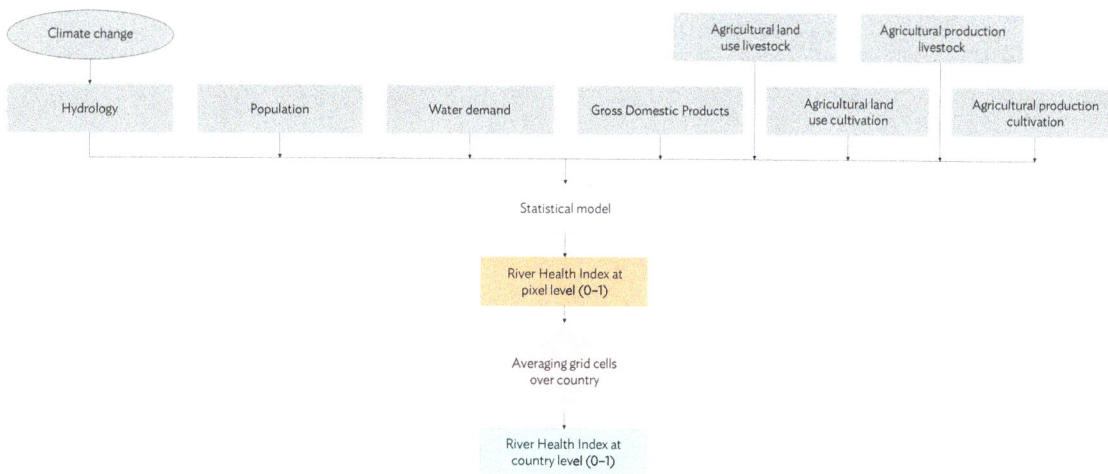

Climate change

Hydrology | Population | Water demand | Gross Domestic Products | Agricultural land use cultivation | Agricultural production cultivation

Agricultural land use livestock | Agricultural production livestock

Statistical model

River Health Index at pixel level (0–1)

Averaging grid cells over country

River Health Index at country level (0–1)

Source: ADB.

The model is pixel based. For each pixel (0.5° Lat/Long – about 50×50 km) at locations with appreciable river flow (based on the City University of New York [CUNY] river network), the "condition" of that cell is calculated under the "pressure" of a number of drivers or threats, as included in Figure 12. These seven drivers (population, water demand, GDP, agricultural land use cultivation, agricultural land use livestock, agricultural production cultivation, agricultural production livestock) are actually surrogates of the 23 drivers used in AWDO 2013.

The statistical model is a generalized least squares multiple regression that relates threat to water security to the driver variables. The model assumes normally distributed errors with a spatial covariance matrix that captures the diluting effect of river flow on threat to water security:

$$Y_i = X\beta + \varepsilon$$

where

- Y_i = the observed RHI from AWDO 2013 in the ith grid cell of the given river;
- $X\beta$ = the matrix of surrogate driver variables, described in Table 33, and the

associated parameter vector containing the regression coefficients; and

- ε = error term which is normally distributed with mean 0 and variance–covariance matrix Σ.

The elements of the variance–covariance matrix are estimated via an exponential covariance model with parameters that estimate the effective range of autocorrelation down the river network.

The impact of upstream grid cells is quantified with a flow-weighted spatial covariance matrix (Peterson, Theobald, and Ver Hoef 2007) which allows the effect of an upstream grid cell to decline with distance and flow (Figure 13). In this way, the RHI at a given grid cell is based on the impact of human activity at that grid cell (via the relationship to the driver variables), plus the RHI upstream, flowing down with river discharge.

The spatial statistical model was fit separately at each river basin that is larger than 24 grid cells. We used variance inflation factors to remove predictor variables that were highly correlated within basins, ensuring a sound basis for the forecasts and avoiding underestimation of the variance parameters for each basin. This resulted in different

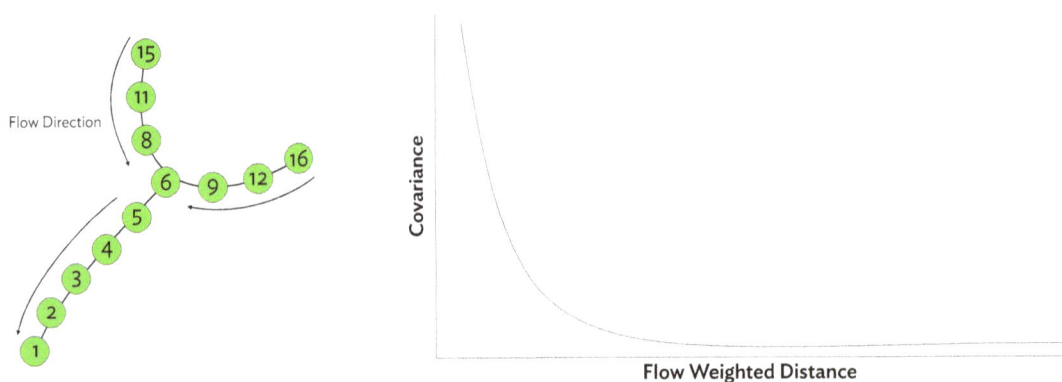

Figure 13: Conceptual Diagram of a River Network and a Spatial Covariance Model

Notes: Each circle in the river network represents a specific grid cell, with an associated label. The estimated water security index is related to the process at that pixel grid cell and some effect of water security flowing down from upstream grid cells. The effect of upstream grid cells declines as the flow-weighted distance between them increases.

Source: Prepared by the International Water Center.

regression relationships across each large basin in the region. A single model for smaller river basins was fit collectively due to the required sample size for the spatial model (see section 7.2.3 for details). The model calculates the river health index (a number between 0 and 1).

7.2.1 Data Source Used

All datasets have been harmonized to a consistent 0.5° (Lat/Long) spatial gridded framework with global extents, to be consistent with Vörösmarty et al. (2010) river threat data. Global data have been subset to the AWDO country extents and river basin country units associated with AWDO countries using the CUNY gridded river networks (Vörösmarty, Federer, and Schloss 1998; Wisser et al. 2010). Due to the 0.5° spatial resolution and the global nature of the gridded threat data and CUNY river network, some smaller Island countries in the AWDO were not included in this analysis. A summary of the data source is given in Table 31.

A. Climate (represented by changes in precipitation and subsequent river flows)

Climate projections from the Inter-Sectoral Impact Model Intercomparison Project (ISI–MIP) (Warszawski et al. 2013) provide the foundation for water flow volumes associated with the contemporary and future threat scenarios. Water flow is estimated at 30° x 30° (longitude x latitude) grid cell resolution using WBM$_{plus}$, a coupled water balance and transport model that simulates the vertical water exchange between the land surface and the atmosphere and the horizontal water transport along a prescribed river network (Vörösmarty, Federer, and Schloss 1998; Wisser et al. 2010). WBM$_{plus}$ was used to calculate components of the hydrological cycle using a time series of climate forcing data from ISI–MIP coupled with land cover and soil characteristics to compute monthly and annual renewable runoff and discharge in each grid cell accounting for precipitation,

evapotranspiration, irrigation, and infiltration to groundwater. Runoff and discharge composites were created at 30-year long-term annual averages across five global climate models (GFDL-ESM2M, HadGEM2-ES, IPSL-CM5A-LR, MIROC-ESM-CHEM, and NorESM1-M) for four representative concentration pathways models (RCPs) (2.6, 4.5, 6.0, and 8.5) representing alternate scenarios of hotter/cooler and wetter/drier climate projections. For AWDO 2016, we use discharge estimates for the RCP 6 scenario only.

B. Population Growth

Contemporary global gridded population was derived from the Global Rural-Urban Mapping Project (CIESIN 2011) rescaled to 30′ (longitude x latitude) grid cell resolution and benchmarked to year 2000. The population was projected to 2010 using the contemporary rescaled GRUMP population dataset and scaling this on a grid cell basis by country-level urban and rural population growth rate projections relative to 2000 from the ISI-MIP Shared Socioeconomic Pathways (SSPs) database.[11] For the KD4 analysis, we chose the "middle-of-the-road" SSP2 scenario, although other scenarios representing more or less aggressive socioeconomic growth and intensification are available from this dataset. Population grids are built for total urban and rural populations at 30′ grid cell resolution for 2010.

C. Water Demand

Contemporary water demand at the grid cell level was calculated as water withdrawals (km³/yr) from the domestic, electricity production, manufacturing, and agriculture sectors for 2010 (Flörke et al. 2013, Warszawski et al. 2013). For future water demand projections, mean annual water withdrawals are the volume of water withdrawals (km³/yr) from the domestic, electricity production, manufacturing, and agriculture sectors from the ISI-MIP SSP2 projections (and where appropriate, RCP 6) for 2025. At the time of this report, water withdrawal

---

[11]   See SSP Database, 2012–2015 at https://tntcat.iiasa.ac.at/SspDb

data were not available from ISI-MIP for any of the other dates in our analysis.

D. Economic Development

Contemporary gridded GDP is taken from the GECON dataset (Nordhaus et al. 2006) rescaled to the 30-minute grid cell resolution and benchmarked to 2005. GDP was projected for 2010 using the contemporary rescaled GECON GDP dataset and scaling this on a grid cell basis by country-level GDP growth from the ISI-MIP SSP2 scenario. This driver captures the impact of general economic activity, including manufacturing and industry, on water security.

E. Agricultural Land Use and Production Change

Data on agricultural land use and production change are derived from the ISI-MIP SSP2 food system simulations and have been developed by colleagues at the International Institute for Applied Systems Analysis. The results presented in this report are based on the use of these variables. Agricultural land use change data include percentage of cultivated and irrigated land in grid cells at 30-minute grid cell resolution for 2000 and 2010. Agricultural production data include gross value of crop and livestock production (GVPC and GVPL, respectively) at international prices

Table 31: Summary of Data Sources Used in the Development of the Statistical Model for the Refined Environmental Water Security Index

Input Data Description	Time Frame	Reference	Data Source
Threat to environmental water security	2000	Vörösmarty et al. (2010)	http://riverthreat.net/data.html
Runoff	2000 2010	Warszawski et al. (2013)	Balazs Fekete, CUNY Environmental CrossRoads Initiative, bfekete@ccny.cuny.edu
Population	2000	CIESIN (2011) (gridded data)	http://sedac.ciesin.columbia.edu/data/collection/grump-v1
	2000 2010	International Institute for Applied Systems Analysis (IIASA), Shared Socioeconomic Pathways (SSPs) database v1.0 (country population growth)	https://secure.iiasa.ac.at/web-apps/ene/SspDb/dsd?Action=htmlpage&page=about
Water demand	2000 2010	Flörke et al. (2013); Warszawski et al. (2013)	Center for Environmental Systems Research
Gross domestic product (GDP)	2000	Nordhaus et al. (2006) (gridded data)	http://gecon.yale.edu (World Bank data for each country provide the basis for this spatially distributed data)
	2000 2010	SSP database v1.0 (country GDP change)	https://secure.iiasa.ac.at/web-apps/ene/SspDb/dsd?Action=htmlpage&page=about
Agricultural land use (cultivation and livestock)	2000 2010	Manuscript in preparation	Guenther Fischer, IIASA
Agricultural production (cultivation, livestock)	2000 2010	Manuscript in preparation	Guenther Fischer, IIASA

Source: ADB.

2004–2006 in grid cells at 30-minute grid cell resolution for 2000 and 2010.

7.2.2 Scoring Table

The river health index is calculated based on the thresholds given in Table 32.

Table 32: Scoring Table for the River Health index

River Health Index		River Health Index Range
1	Bad	≤ 0.22
2	Poor	0.221–0.36
3	Moderate	0.361–0.54
4	Good	0.541–0.71
5	Excellent	> 0.71

Source: ADB.

7.2.3 Changes from the Asian Water Development Outlook 2013

The approach used in AWDO 2013 was based on the approach of Vörösmarty et al. (2010) in their global-scale analysis of threats to river ecosystems. Their index was based on 23 drivers of threat to environmental water security for biodiversity, which was transformed to create the RHI that was the basis for KD4 in AWDO 2013. The majority of these drivers are not being updated in a consistent manner, complicating the use of this index for future AWDO reports. As such, IWC has developed an approach based on a statistical model that defines threat to environmental water security, and subsequently the RHI, with a smaller number of drivers that are being developed and updated by several stakeholders. This approach is underpinned by the known relationships between various stressors (e.g., pollution loading, catchment disturbance, and water resource use) on water quality or ecosystem health more broadly. As such, the modeled river basin "threat" indicator is derived

from widely available spatial datasets, is routed through stream networks, and provides an inverse measure of ecosystem health (see Appendix 5 of AWDO 2013).

The newly developed threat index is based on a statistical model approach, and the subsequently refined RHI represents a closely related but redefined index of KD4 from AWDO 2013. As it is highly unlikely that all 23 drivers will be updated consistently in the future, the statistical model approach provides an avenue to redefine the RHI in a manner that closely reflects the original index but can be updated as required for future AWDO efforts. As the statistical model effectively redefines the RHI, some differences may be expected between the original RHI, the KD4 index, and the modeled index developed here. As such, any assessments of ongoing changes to environmental water security in a given country should be made by comparing forecast changes to modeled KD4 index scores.

The majority of the original 23 drivers that contributed to the original RHI were agricultural in nature (e.g., cropland and livestock density); the surrogate drivers we have assembled represent those processes (Table 33). In addition to the surrogate drivers for agricultural processes, population and GDP represent the urban and industrial processes in the original drivers (e.g., impervious surfaces). In Table 33, the relevant surrogate driver(s) for the RHI in AWDO 2016 is shaded in gray for each driver.

7.2.4 Missing Data

The KD4 methodology cannot be applied for the small island states and no results could be calculated for these. KD4 identified two categories:

- Small island economies whose RHI can be reasonably estimated based on population and GDP alone: the Cook Islands; Hong Kong, China; Palau; Samoa; and Tonga

Table 33: Original 23 Drivers of the Asian Water Development Outlook 2013 versus the 7 New Drivers of the Asian Water Development Outlook 2016

Theme	Driver	Population	GDP	% area irrigation	GVPC	% area livestock	GVPL	Water withdrawals
Catchment disturbance	Cropland							
	Livestock density							
	Impervious surfaces							
	Wetland disconnectivity							
Pollution	Soil salinization							
	Phosphorus loading							
	Pesticide loading							
	Organic loading							
	Thermal alteration							
	Nitrogen loading							
	Mercury deposition							
	Sediment loading							
	Potential acidification							
Water resource development	Dam density							
	Consumptive water loss							
	Agricultural water stress							
	River fragmentation							
	Human water stress							
	Flow disruption							
Biotic factors	Non-native fish (%)							
	Non-native fish (#)							
	Fishing pressure							
	Aquaculture pressure							

GDP = gross domestic product, GVPC = gross value of crop production, GVPL = gross value of livestock production.
Source: ADB.

- Small island countries for which no RHI should be derived because they have no rivers to speak of: Kiribati, the Maldives, the Marshall Islands, the Federated States of Micronesia, Nauru, and Tuvalu

It was decided that AWDO 2016 will not make an estimate for the RHI score of these economies. Instead, expert opinions on the overall score of KD4 were used (see section 7.5 for how this was done).

7.3 Subindicator: Flow Alteration

A major impact on the riverine environment across the world is the alteration of the natural flow regime (Bunn and Arthington 2002). Altered hydrology may come from direct extraction, which may or may not be offset by return flows, or physical infrastructure such as dams and weirs. While the resultant hydrologic alteration often produces tangible benefits for humans, such as reliable water supply for consumption, agriculture, and flood mitigation, these are often in the context of impaired ecosystem health and integrity. Such flow regimes may feature reduced flow variability or even entail a completely reversed seasonality with high flow events occurring in the low flow season to provide water for irrigation (Crook et al. 2015). Such changes are typically detrimental to in-stream biota given the dramatic changes from the natural flow regime in which they evolved (Bunn and Arthington 2002). As such, we have developed a simple indicator that integrates the spatial and temporal extent of flow alteration for each country in the region as a measure of the impact of existing infrastructure development on the environment. The index of flow alteration represents the number of months per year where total discharge differs more than 20% from pristine levels.

7.3.1 Data Source Used

The derivation of the indicator that reflected the spatial and temporal extent of hydrologic alteration was more straightforward than the threats to environmental water security. The derivation used modeled river flow under five different general circulation models comparing modeled pristine (unaltered) and disturbed conditions (Wisser et al. 2010). An analysis of the difference between these two components provided an avenue for assessing the extent of hydrologic alteration within each country.

As the hydrologic data are spatially distributed, the index is calculated as the proportion of grid cells in a country where the observed monthly discharge is more than 20% different from pristine discharge at least once a year. The analysis was run for each of the five general circulation models and the average of the five outcomes was calculated as an index of the alteration. This metric has been developed as a presumptive indicator of moderate ecological impact on river flows (Richter et al. 2012). It accounts for the impact of too little flow when flows are reduced by the presence of large dams or direct

abstraction without return flows, and too much flow due to augmentation from interbasin transfers, both of which can have negative impacts on in-stream biota (Stewart-Koster and Bunn 2016). This is subsequently expressed as a percentage to indicate the spatial extent of hydrologic alteration in the country.

7.3.2 Scoring Table

The percentages are converted to the 1-5 categorical values according to the equivalent thresholds to the RHI in Table 34.

Table 34: Scoring Table for Flow Alteration

Flow Alteration Index		Range (%)
1	Bad	≥ 71
2	Poor	54.1–70.9
3	Moderate	36.1–54
4	Good	22.1–36
5	Excellent	≤ 22

Source: ADB.

7.3.3 Missing Data

The indicator of hydrologic alteration was only calculated for regions with appreciable flowing surface water. As such, dry regions such as central Australia and central People's Republic of China are not included in the calculations for those countries. For countries with areas of no appreciable flow, the indicator represents the proportion only of grid cells with appreciable flow that are altered hydrologically. This has the effect of excluding arid regions from the calculation of the spatial extent of hydrological alteration as there is little or no effective flow to alter in these regions.

In addition to the exclusion of arid regions from the indicator, it is not calculated for countries with no surface flow at all, such as the small island countries in the Pacific. Consequently, as there is effectively no flowing water in these countries, no index of hydrological alteration is calculated for them (see section 7.5 for how this is taken into account).

7.4 Subindicator: Environmental Management

An important aspect of environmental water security is the institutional capacity and willingness of each country to reduce and prevent environmental degradation. Numerous pressures on river systems can be offset with appropriate mitigation measures that prevent associated reductions in river health, which are possible with strong governance. It is widely understood that what happens on the land that is drained by a given river, be it agricultural, industrial, or urban development, contributes in large part to the in-stream river condition (Allan 2004). As such, we have developed an indicator of governance for each country which comprises measures of environmental protection in each country.

There are four subindicators that comprise the indicator of governance, which have been retrieved from the Yale Environmental Performance Index (EPI) for 2014 (at epi.yale.edu). These subindicators represent the extent to which the country has gone to protect its terrestrial environment and reduce harmful pollutants to the landscape, and subsequently the surface water systems. They are

(i)   wastewater treatment,
(ii) pesticide regulation,
(iii) forest loss since 2000, and
(iv) terrestrial protected areas.

These have been developed specifically as subcomponents of the EPI, which is an indicator of overall environmental performance. They have been selected as indicators of governance for environmental water security as they represent processes that are known to have direct influences on the aquatic ecosystem condition. Each of these subindicators is scored as a percentage, and the same thresholds defined for the indicator of hydrologic alteration (Table 34) are used for each subindicator to define category outcomes.

The final indicator for governance is calculated simply as the median of the four subindicators to derive an overall governance score ranging from 1 to 5.

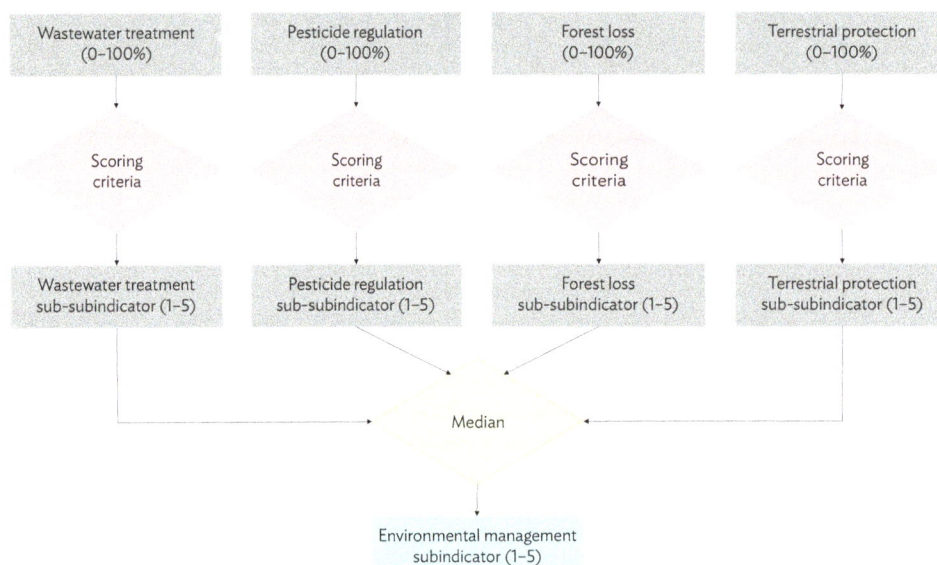

Figure 14: Calculation Approach for the Environmental Management Indicator

Source: ADB.

7.4.1 Data Sources Used

All four indexes used are taken from the Yale EPI (all on a percent scale).

Wastewater Treatment

The subindicator for wastewater treatment was developed by the EPI to provide an assessment of the extent of wastewater treatment in a country, which acts to improve the quality of receiving waters. The index is based on data from several agencies including national ministries, the Organisation for Economic Co-operation and Development, the UN Statistics Division, the Food and Agriculture Organization of the UN, and Pinsent Masons Water Yearbook (Hsu et al. 2014). It combines the amount of wastewater treated in the sewerage system with the population connected to the sewerage system to derive a percentage outcome:

WW_treatment = % of treated × % of population connected to sewerage system

This percentage is then converted into the five categories using the thresholds in Table 35.

Pesticide Regulation

The subindicator for pesticides was included as evidence of a country's willingness and capacity to reduce the extent of harmful contaminants reaching aquatic systems. It consists of two components: The first is the status of the country as a signatory to the Stockholm Convention to protect human health and the environment from the "Dirty Dozen" persistent organic pollutants.[12] The second is the banned status, or otherwise, of each of these 12 persistent organic pollutants within the legislative framework of the country. Up to three points toward the subindicator are awarded for signing and/or ratifying the Stockholm Convention and a subsequent two points are awarded for the banning of each of the "Dirty Dozen" persistent organic pollutants. The score is set to a maximum of 25 and each country's result is then converted to a percentage for the EPI (Hsu et al. 2014). This percentage is subsequently converted into the five categories using the thresholds in Table 35.

Forest Loss since 2000

The subindicator that covers deforestation represents an important process that is known to harm aquatic ecosystems (Allan 2004). Native vegetation plays an important role in regulating the flow of water, nutrients, and materials to the streams that drain the landscape. The loss of vegetation can increase nutrient and sediment loads to the stream as well as increase the velocity of runoff and subsequently the declining arm of the hydrograph. Such physical and hydrological alterations to the stream can have detrimental impacts to aquatic biota. As such, the loss of forest cover over a decade provides an indicator of a country's capacity to protect its terrestrial resources, thereby preventing detrimental impacts on its aquatic systems. The indicator simply quantifies the percent change in forest covered land from 2000 to 2012. Once again, the percentage value is converted to the five categories according to the thresholds in Table 35.

Terrestrial Protected Areas

The final subindicator for the governance component of KD4 focuses on the legislative framework for landscape protection within each country. The subindicator assesses the protection of the various biomes within a country weighted by the proportion of a country's territory each biome occupies. This provides an avenue to quantify the degree to which terrestrial habitat is protected, thereby preventing detrimental impacts

---

12   These are the 12 persistent organic pollutants that have been recognized as causing adverse effects on humans and the ecosystem and these can be places in 3 categories: (i) Pesticides: aldrin, chlordane, DDT, dieldrin, endrin, heptachlor, hexachlorobenzene, mirex, toxaphene; (ii) Industrial chemicals: hexachlorobenzene, polychlorinated biphenyls (PCBs); and, (iii) By-products: hexachlorobenzene; polychlorinated dibenzo-p-dioxins and polychlorinated dibenzofurans (PCDD/PCDF), and PCBs. Source: http://chm.pops.int/Convention/ThePOPs/The12InitialPOPs/tabid/296/Default.aspx accessed on 1 August 2016.

to environmental water security. As with each of the subindicators for the governance indicator, the thresholds in Table 35 are used to define the five categories for the subindicator.

7.4.2 Scoring Table

The environmental management index is calculated based on the thresholds shown in Table 35.

Table 35: Scoring Table for the Environmental Management Index

Environmental Management Index		% Range
1	Bad	< 22
2	Poor	22–36
3	Moderate	36.1–54
4	Good	54.1–70.9
5	Excellent	≥ 71

Source: ADB.

7.4.3 Missing Data

The availability of data for the governance indicator was generally similar as for the RHI, with some of the small island countries missing all subindicators. In other countries, such as Tajikistan and Tonga, only the data for subindicator for forest loss were missing with those for all other subindicators available.

Where all subindicators were missing, we were unable to provide an estimate of the governance regime for aquatic systems. Where only data for forest loss were missing, the governance indicator was calculated as the median of the three available subindicators.

7.5 How Did We Deal with Missing Data for Environmental Water Security and with Countries without Rivers?

As explained in section 7.2.4, the KD4 methodology cannot be applied for some of the small island countries because they have no rivers to speak of. Still, for comparison reasons, it was decided that those countries will also receive a KD4 score, which will be estimated by experts and should be seen as a general score on the state of the aquatic ecosystem in the country. For some others, scores for flow and/or governance were missing. Most of the cases of missing data were small island states again, for which we have made use of expert opinions (refer to Appendix 2). The following assumptions were made:

Without rivers

- Kiribati: EO – 3 points (out of 15)
- Maldives: No EO available, same score as AWDO 2013 – 12 points
- Marshall Islands: EO – 9 points
- Federated States of Micronesia: EO – 12 points
- Nauru: EO – 15 points (max), after internal discussion reduced to 12 points
- Tuvalu: EO – 12 points

Missing data on flow and governance

- Hong Kong, China: No EO available, same score as AWDO 2013 – 9 points
- Palau: EO 12 points, considering available data reduced to 11 points
- Samoa: EO 12 points, considering available data reduced to 10 points
- Tonga: EO 6 points.

7.6 Overall Assessment Environmental Water Security

The new methodology of KD4 is a major improvement compared with the one used for AWDO 2013. The modeling exercise is made much simpler, requiring less data. The inclusion of the new flow regulation subindicator adds another dimension to river health. Finally, adding governance as a subindicator means that the KD4 score can now also be improved by taking action.

A major issue on KD4 is that the score for the RHI can only be determined by using the model developed by the World Resources Institute. All other key dimensions can be calculated based on data only, using straightforward spreadsheets. Conversely, KD4 is the only key dimension that can be applied easily at the river basin scale. This can be done by simply adding the cells of the particular basin. The use of the model also enables making projections.

The World Resources Institute anticipates submitting a publication on the model (together with Vörösmarty, Wiberg, and others) toward the middle of 2016. After the publication is accepted in a journal, the institute intends to make the code for the model publicly available.

8 Key Dimension 5: Resilience to Water-Related Disasters

Key dimension 5 (KD5) describes the capacity of a country to cope with and recover from the impacts of water-related disasters. It is based on the performance of three subindicators that describe the resilience against

- floods and windstorms,
- drought, and
- storm surges and coastal floods.

The approach to KD5 in AWDO 2016 is the same as the approach followed in AWDO 2013.

The KD5 approach has originally been developed by the International Centre for Water Hazard and Risk Management (ICHARM) in Japan.

8.1 Assessment Framework

The assessment framework for KD5 is illustrated in Figure 15.

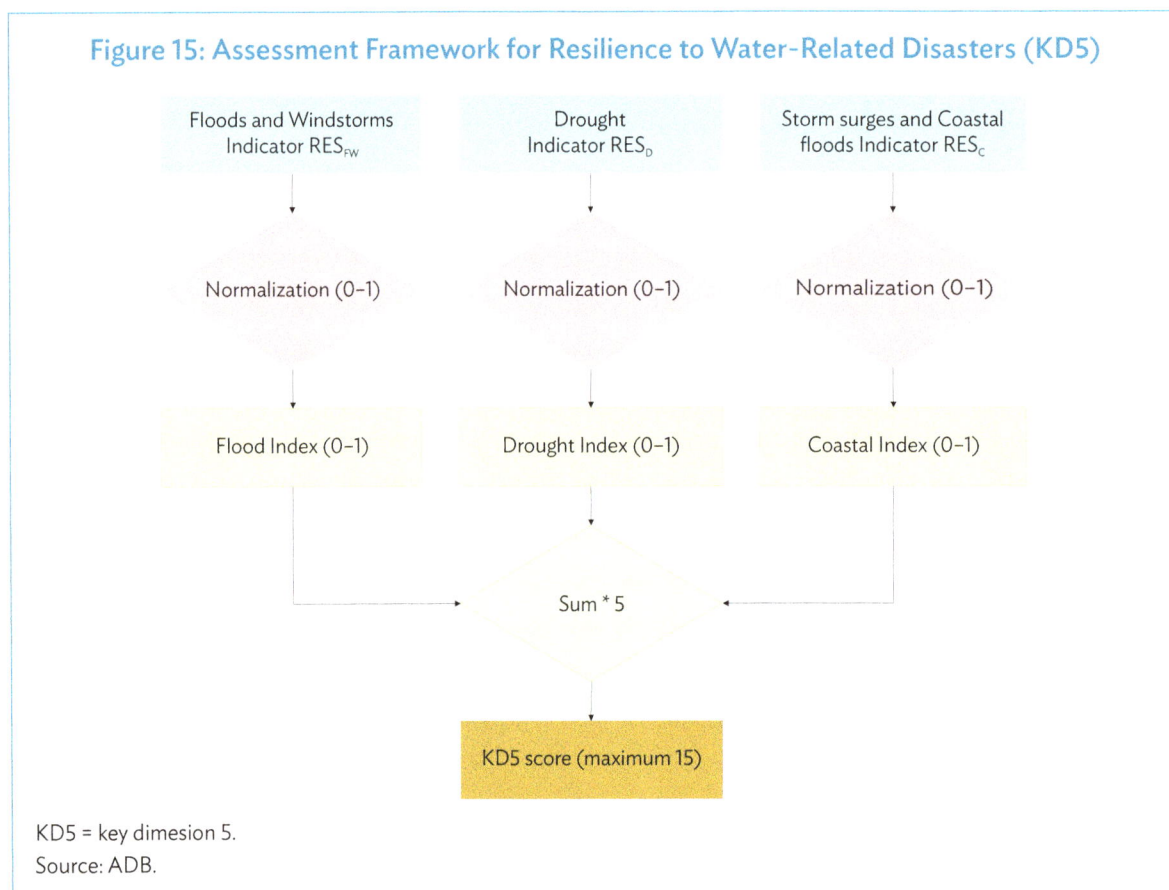

Figure 15: Assessment Framework for Resilience to Water-Related Disasters (KD5)

KD5 = key dimesion 5.
Source: ADB.

All three subindicators are scored on a scale of 0–1. The approach how this was done is explained in the next sections. The total KD5 score is the sum of these three subindicator scores. To express this score in an order of magnitude of the other key dimensions, the sum is multiplied by 5, which results in a maximum score of 15.

This assessment framework is basically the same as the one used for AWDO 2013.

8.2 Approach Followed for the Calculation of the Resilience Subindicators

To determine the score for the three resilience indicators, a specific procedure was followed. This is the same for all three subindicators and is illustrated in Figure 16.

Figure 16: Steps Followed in Determining the Resilience Subindicators

		Flood and windstorms (FW)	Drought (D)	Storm Surge / Coastal Flooding (C)
Step 1: Basic data + standardization (0–1)	E Exposure	Population density, urban and population growth rates	Population density, urban and population growth rates	Population density, population growth rates, % are below 10m
	V_B Basic Vulnerability	Governance, poverty, ODA, infant mortality, deforestration	Governance, poverty, ODA, infant mortality, agricultural GDP	Governance, poverty, ODA, deforestation, infant mortality
	C_H Hard Coping capacity	GDP, reservoir capacity	GDP, reservoir capacity	GDP, paved road density
	C_S Soft Coping capacity	Literacy, education, TV, mobiles, economic growth	Literacy, education, TV, mobiles, economic growth	Literacy, education, TV, mobiles, economic growth
Step 2: Determine joint score for E, V, C	Combined score (sum)	E_{FW}, VB_{FW}, C_{FW}	E_D, VB_D, C_D	E_C, VB_C, C_C
Step 3: Calculate Vulnerability V Resilience Res	Vulnerability	$V_{FW}=(E_{FW}+VB_{FW})*(1-C_{FW}/C_{FWmax})$	$V_D=(E_D+VB_D)*(1-C_D/C_{Dmax})$	$V_C=(E_C+VB_C)*(1-C_C/C_{Cmax})$
	Resilience	$Res_{FW} = 1/V_{FW}$	$Res_D = 1/V_D$	$Res_C = 1/V_C$
		Floods and Windstorms Indicator Res_{FW}	Drought Indicator Res_D	Storm surges and Coastal floods Indicator Res_C

GDP = gross domestic product, m = meter, ODA = official development assistance.
Source: ADB.

Step 1: Processing basic data

- Collect data on factors of the indicators, exposure (E), basic vulnerability (VB), and coping capacities (CS and CH) (see Table 36)
- (Log) Standardize these factors between 0 and 1

Step 2: Calculate averages and set CMAX

- Calculate the values of H, E, VB, and coping capacity (C)

= sum of normalized factors divided/corrected for the number of factors in each indicator (to make them comparable)

Table 36: Subindicators and Sub-subindicators Used for Resilience to Water-Related Disasters

Sub-subindicator Category \ Subindicator Category	Floods and Windstorms	Drought	Storm Surge/ Coastal Flooding
Hazard (H)*	1. Maximum weekly average precipitation (millimeter) 2. Cyclone proneness (hits and magnitude) 3. Frequency (>100 millimeter/day rainfall)	1. Number of consecutive dry days (<5 millimeter rainfall) 2. Dryland as percentage of total area	1. Cyclone susceptibility (hits and magnitude 2. Coastal line length/land area
Exposure (E)	1. Population density 2. Urban population growth rate 3. Population growth rate		1. Population density 2. **Population proportion of lowland area (below 10 meters) (%)** 3. Population growth rate
Basic vulnerability (VB)	1. Governance (likelihood of corruption) 2. Percentage of population below $1/day consumption 3. Net official development assistance as percent of gross net income 4. **Deforestation rate** 5. Infant mortality rate (1,000 live births)	1. Governance (likelihood of corruption) 2. Percentage of population below $1/day consumption 3. Net official development assistance as percent of gross net income 4. **Agricultural gross production per gross domestic product (%)** 5. Infant mortality rate (1,000 live births)	1. Governance (likelihood of corruption) 2. Percentage of population below $1/day consumption 3. Net official development assistance as percent of gross net income 4. Infant mortality rate (1,000 live births)
Hard coping capacity (CH)	1. Potential investment density (gross domestic product per area) 2. Total reservoir capacity per area		1. Potential investment density (gross domestic product per area) 2. **Infrastructure (paved road density)**
Soft coping capacity (CS)	1. Literacy ratio 2. Education (enrolment ratio) 3. Information (television receivers per 1,000 inhabitants) 4. Information (mobile phone subscriptions) 5. Economic growth (gross domestic savings)		

Notes:
The data printed in bold are the data specific for that subindicator.
* Data on H are not needed to determine the key dimension.
Source: ADB.

- Set maximum coping capacity (CMAX) at 1.5 x maximum value of present capacity

Step 3: Calculate vulnerability and resilience

- Calculate vulnerability (V) as a function of E, VB, and C:
$V = (E + V_B) \times (1 - C/C_{MAX})$
- Define resilience (Res) as the ability of a system to recover from the effects of a hazard:
$Res = 1 / V$
- Normalize the resilience score to fall between 0 and 1.

Note that in this procedure the calculation of risk is not included. Risk is hazard multiplied by vulnerability, so R = H x V. In preparing AWDO 2013, it was decided that KD5 would focus on resilience to disasters and that that the occurrence of extreme events would not play a role in determining KD5. This means also that the data on H does not need to be collected.

Figure 16 gives an overview of the data elements (sub-subindicators) used for the three subindicators. More detail is given in the next section for the three subindicators.

8.3 Subindicators: Floods/Windstorms, Drought, and Storm Surge/Coastal Flooding

Table 36 shows that all three subindicators have many sub-subindicators in common. For that reason, the three subindicators are described jointly.

8.3.1 Data Sources Used

This section describes first the indicators that are common to all three subindicators, followed by those of the specific subindicators (Tables 37–41).

8.3.2 Scoring Table

To summarize the scoring approach that was followed for KD5 as already explained:

- All data were standardized between 0 and 1. The highest value was given the score of 1 and the other values were standardized by dividing their value by the highest value.
- The joint score of the parameters (E, V, and C) was determined by averaging.
- Vulnerability (V) and resilience (R) were calculated.

This approach means that no banding has taken place for KD5. The score is the result of a straightforward calculation.

8.3.3 Changes from the Asian Water Development Outlook 2013

The methodology of KD5 in AWDO 2016 is exactly the same as used in AWDO 2013. Differences in the score of KD5 for 2016 compared with 2013 are the result of

- use of more recent data,
- some adjustments in the handling of nonrelevant parameters in the calculations, and
- correction of some errors in the (rather complex) spreadsheets from ICHARM.

The first and last bullets are self-explanatory. The second bullet is about how to "score" a sub-subindicator for a certain country when this indicator is not relevant for that country. This is not specific for KD5 but applies for KD2 and partly for KD4 as well. An example is the storm surge and coastal flooding subindicator for landlocked countries such as Bhutan, Mongolia, and Nepal. Another example is the agricultural water security indicator for city economies such as Singapore and Hong Kong, China. In AWDO 2013, this was not handled in a consistent manner. In some cases, they were given the maximum score (leading to an

Table 37: Data Sources Used for General Sub-subindicators for Resilience to Water-Related Disasters

Sub-subindicator	Unit	Year of Data	Data Source
Exposure			
Population density	#/km²	2012	ESCAP Online Statistical Database
Urban growth rate	%	2012	ESCAP Online Statistical Database
Population growth rate	%	2012	ESCAP Online Statistical Database
Vulnerability			
Governance (corruption)	index	2014	Transparency International https://www.transparency.org/cpi2014/results
% people below $1.25/day	%	2013	ESCAP Online Statistical Database
% net ODA to gross net income	%	2012	World Bank Database (World Development Indicators)
Infant mortality rate/1,000 births	#	2013	ESCAP Online Statistical Database
Hard coping capacity			
Pot. investment density		2014	World Bank Database (World Development Indicators)
Soft coping capacity			
Literacy ratio	%	2015 est.	Central Intelligence Agency World Factbook
Education (enrollment ratio)	%	2014	United Nations Development Programme Human Development Report
Information (TV/1,000 inh.)	#	2003	NationMaster.com Australia
Information (mobile/100 inh.)	#	2013	Millennium Development Goals Database (United Nations Statistics Division)
Econ. growth/ gross domestic saving		2013	World Bank Database (World Development Indicators)

ESCAP = Economic and Social Commission for Asia and the Pacific, km² = square kilometer, ODA = official development assistance.
Source: ADB.

Table 38: Data Source Used for Floods and Windstorms Sub-subindicators

Sub-subindicator	Unit	Year of Data	Data Source
Deforestation rate	%	2005–2010	FAO – Global Forest Resources Assessment 2010

FAO = Food and Agriculture Organization of the United Nations.
Source: ADB.

Table 39: Data Source Used for Floods, Windstorms, and Drought Sub-subindicators

Sub-subindicator	Unit	Year of Data	Data Source
Reservoir capacity per area	m³/km²	2012	Total Dam or Reservoir Capacity: Global Reservoir and Dam (GRanD) Database

km² = square kilometer, m³ = cubic meter.
Source: ADB.

Table 40: Data Source Used for Drought Sub-subindicators

Sub-subindicator	Unit	Year of Data	Data Source
Agricultural part of gross domestic product	%	2014	World Bank Database (World Development Indicators)

Source: ADB.

Table 41: Data Sources Used for Storm Surges and Coastal Flooding Sub-subindicators

Sub-subindicator	Unit	Year of Data	Data Source
Population proportion living in area below 5 meters	%	2000	World Bank Database (World Development Indicators)
Infrastructure (paved road density)		2006–2015	Central Intelligence Agency World Factbook

Source: ADB.

overestimate); in other cases, they were given the minimum score (leading to an underestimate of the subindicator). In AWDO 2016, these parameters have been ignored and the score of the subindicator was based on the remaining sub-subindicators only.

8.3.4 Missing Data

Data on various sub-subindicators of KD5 are missing for Afghanistan, Bhutan, Myanmar, and Timor-Leste, as well as for the small island states of the Cook Islands, the Maldives, the Marshall Islands, the Federated States of Micronesia, Nauru, Palau, Solomon Islands, and Tuvalu. Expert opinions (EO) have been used to determine the scores of these missing data.

The status of the scores used for the missing data as of 21 April 2016 is as follows:

- Afghanistan: estimate AWDO team (1, 1, -); total 3 points (out of 15)

- Bhutan: estimate by Lance Gore of ADB (2, 2, -); total 6 points (out of 15)
- Myanmar: estimate by Tjitte Nauta of Deltares (2, 1, 1); total 4 points (out of 15)
- Cook Islands: EO followed for all three subindicators (see Appendix 2)
- Maldives: estimate AWDO team (1, 1, 1); total 3 points (out of 15)
- Marshall Islands: EO followed for all three subindicators (see Appendix 2)
- Federated States of Micronesia: EO followed for all three subindicators (see Appendix 2)
- Nauru: EO followed for all three subindicators (see Appendix 2)
- Palau: EO followed for all three subindicators (see Appendix 2)
- Solomon Islands: EO followed for all three subindicators (see Appendix 2)
- Timor-Leste: EO followed for all three subindicators (see Appendix 2)
- Tuvalu: EO followed for all three subindicators (see Appendix 2)

8.4 Overall Assessment of Resilience to Water-Related Disasters in the Asian Water Development Outlook 2016

The basic methodology for KD5 in AWDO 2016 has remained the same compared with AWDO 2013. Applying the approach with new AWDO 2016 data resulted in a number of observations:

- The first is that the hazard itself (the number and intensity of storms, etc.) is not included in the indicator. What is scored is the capacity of a country to deal with hazards, its resilience. This can result in low scores for KD5 in countries where hazards are low because they do not have to invest in resilience. At the same time, the subindicators used (see Table 36) barely include actual measures to reduce the impacts of hazards. Most of the subindicators describe the general development stage of the country and hardly differ between the three subindicators.

- The second observation is that KD5 is very data intensive. Including the hazard would make it even more data intensive.

- The third observation is that the standardization approach (between 0 and 1) can give strange results if a country has a clear outlier value. In such a case, the scores of all other countries are pushed down. The banding approach as used in the other key dimensions seems more appropriate.

- Finally, it is recommended to further clarify the definitions of vulnerability and resilience and make them more compliant with international scientific definitions.

9 National Water Security Index and National Water Security Level

The National Water Security Index (NWSI) measures how far countries have progressed toward national water security. The NWSI combines the results of the five key dimensions. As the scores of the individual key dimensions are not directly comparable (the maximum scores are different), an adjustment is needed to combine them into the NWSI. This is illustrated in Figure 17.

The NWSI is used to determine the national water security (NWS) level. This NWS level distinguishes between five stages as explained in section 2.4 and ranges from hazardous (level 1) to model (level 5). The scoring table as already given in Table 2 is summarized in Table 42. It also includes the corresponding scaling numbers of the 20- and 5-point scales.

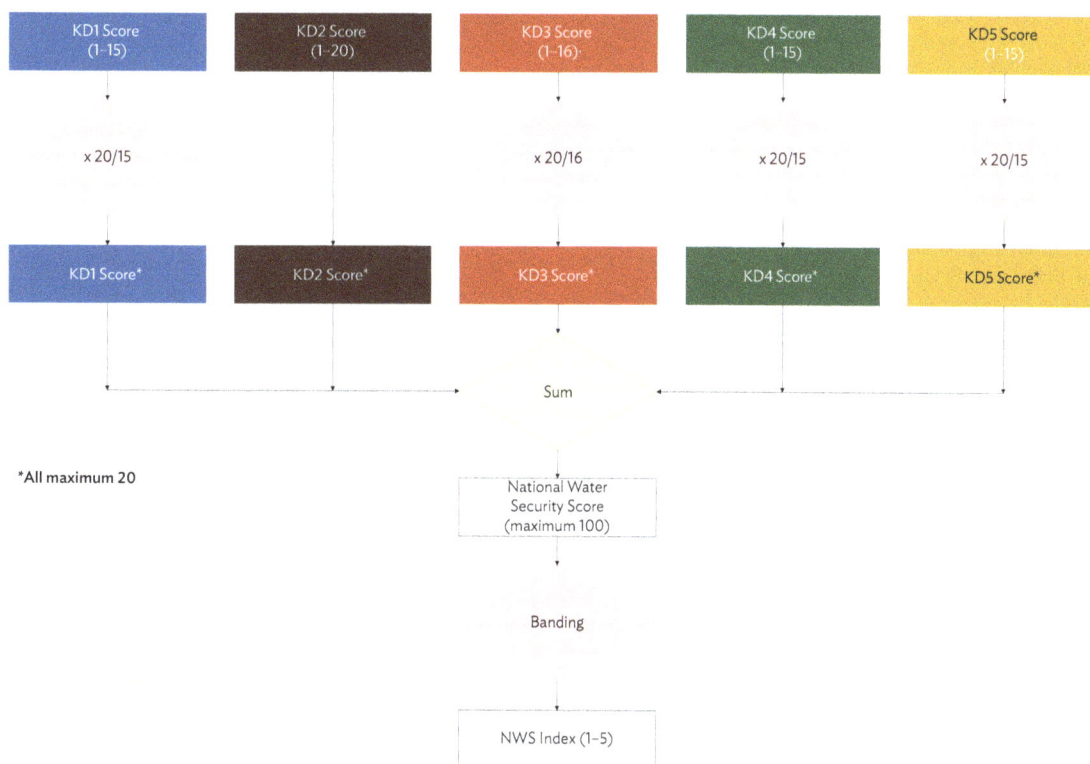

Figure 17: Calculation Procedure for the National Water Security Index and National Water Security Level

KD = key dimension, NWS = national water security.
Source: ADB.

Table 42: Scoring Table for National Water Security Level

Level	Index 100-Point Scale	Index 20-Point Scale	Index 5-Point Scale	Stage
5	≥96	≥19.2	≥4.8	Model
4	76 < 96	15.2 < 19.2	3.8 < 4.8	Effective
3	56 < 76	11.2 < 15.2	2.8 < 3.8	Capable
2	36 < 56	7.2 < 11.2	1.8 < 2.8	Engaged
1	0 < 36	0 < 7.2	0 < 1.8	Hazardous

Source: ADB.

The scoring approach for the NWSI in AWDO 2016 is fundamentally different than in AWDO 2013. In AWDO 2013, the results of each key dimensions were first translated into a key dimension index (on a scale of 1–5). Each key dimension used its own banding for this. The NWS score in AWDO 2013 was the sum of the key dimension index values. The AWDO 2016 approach is favored as it keeps the full information (scores) of the key dimension results.

10 General Assessment of the Methodological Approach for the Asian Water Development Outlook 2016

The methodology of AWDO 2016 described in this report is a major improvement of the approach used for AWDO 2013. Based on the experience with AWDO 2013, we introduced several refinements in the methodological framework of AWDO. The following is an overview of all the changes:

- Household water security (KD1): adjustment of calculation approach to address the redefinition by WHO of the hygiene subindicator (DALY)
- Economic water security (KD2): inclusion of an additional subindicator (broad economy) and redesign of the calculation approach of the other subindicators, including the use of other data sources
- Urban water security (KD3): small adjustment of the scoring methodology (less weight to the river health subindicator) and some minor changes to the calculation of the wastewater and drainage indices
- Environmental water security (KD4): redesign of the river health subindicator and addition of two other subindicators (flow alteration and governance)
- Resilience to water-related disasters (KD5): small adjustments on how the coastal storm surges subindicator is taken into account in landlocked countries.

An important change in the methodology is also how AWDO 2016 scores its results. AWDO 2013 was based on scoring on a 1–5 scale (see Table 2) for the key dimensions and NWSI. In AWDO 2016, the results for the key dimensions are scored on a

1–20 scale while the NWSI is the sum of the KDs on a 1–100 scale. In cases where KDs and NWSI are expressed in the 5 stages of national water security, a uniform banding has been used. In AWDO 2013 each KD used an own defined banding that was different from the banding of the NWSI.

The impacts of the differences in the methodology and data sources have been investigated by recalculation of AWDO 2013 using the new methodology. The results of this analysis are described in Appendix 3. The analysis shows that the results are sufficiently comparable to allow drawing conclusions on the differences between AWDO 2016 and AWDO 2103. Some caution should be exercised though; the different approach and the use of other data sources do in some cases impact the results.

A recurrent discussion on the five key dimensions of AWDO is the perceived "double counting" of specifying urban water security as a separate key dimension. The indicators that compose KD3 are also included in other key dimensions (water supply and sanitation in KD1, flooding in KD5, and river health in KD4). Appendix 4 describes a sensitivity analysis that was carried out on the influence of the "double counting" on the NWS level and the relative position of the AWDO countries. The appendix shows that KD3 indeed influences the results somewhat, but the main messages that AWDO 2016 conveys do not change significantly.

The methodology of AWDO should be seen as a concept in development. AWDO 2016 is a further refinement over AWDO 2013. The next versions of AWDO may consider further refinements. Based on the experience with AWDO 2016, the following points of attention are worth mentioning:

- The small islands states need a separate approach. KD4 is not applicable, while the applicability of KD2 and KD3 is also questionable for small island states.
- There is a need for regional differentiation within countries. For large countries such as the People's Republic of China, India, Indonesia, and/or countries with major regional differences (e.g., Mongolia), a more differentiated approach is preferred.
- Similarly, one might consider following a river basin approach.

With respect to the present methodology, the following points of attention are noteworthy:

- KD1: consider the distinction of urban–rural and rich–poor; maybe redefine the subindicators somewhat to make them comparable to the ones used to monitor Sustainable Development Goal targets 6.1 (water for all) and 6.2 (sanitation and hygiene for all)
- KD2: include renewable water availability (surface water and groundwater)
- KD3: address the double counting issue
- KD4: simplify the computational approach, making it accessible for others
- KD5: simplify the approach and include the hazard

References

Allan, J. D. 2004. Landscapes and Riverscapes: The Influence of Land Use on Stream Ecosystems. *Annual Review of Ecology and Systematics* 35: 257–284.

Asia-Pacific Center for Water Security (APCWS). 2015. Final Report Key Dimension 1 (Household Water Security) of AWDO 2016. Tsinghua University, Beijing, People's Republic of China.

Asian Development Bank (ADB). 2015a. Statistical Database System Online. https://sdbs.adb.org/sdbs/ (accessed on 15 Oct 2015).

———. 2015b. Basic Statistics (2006, 2008, and 2014). http://www.adb.org/publications/series/basic-statistics (accessed on 15 Oct 2015).

———. 2015c. Key Indicators for Asia and the Pacific (2013 and 2014). http://www.adb.org/publications/key-indicators-asia-and-pacific-2014 (accessed on 15 Oct 2015).

Brown, R., N. Keath, and T. Wong. 2009. Urban Water Management in Cities: Historical, Current and Future Regimes. *Water Science and Technology* 59(5): 847–855.

Bunn, S.E., and A.H. Arthington. 2002). Basic Principles and Ecological Consequences of Altered Flow Regimes for Aquatic Biodiversity. *Environmental Management* 30(4): 492–507.

Center for International Earth Science Information Network (CIESIN). 2011. Columbia University, International Food Policy Research Institute (IFPRI), The World Bank, and Centro Internacional de Agricultura Tropical (CIAT). Global Rural-Urban Mapping Project, Version 1 (GRUMPv1): Urban Extents Grid. Palisades, NY: NASA Socioeconomic Data and Applications Center (SEDAC). http://dx.doi.org/10.7927/H4GH9FVG (accessed 2012).

Crook, D.A., et al. 2015. Human Effects on Ecological Connectivity in Aquatic Ecosystems: Integrating Scientific Approaches to Support Management and Mitigation. *Science of the Total Environment* 534: 52–64.

Economic and Social Commission for Asia and the Pacific (ESCAP). 2015. ESCAP Statistical Database. http://www.unescap.org/stat/data/ (retrieved on 26 Oct 2015).

EM-DAT. 2015. *The International Disaster Database, Centre for Research on the Epidemiology of Disasters (CRED)*. Retrieved from: http://www.emdat.be/database

Eriyagama N., V. Smakhtin, and N. Gamage. 2009. Mapping Drought Patterns and Impacts: A Global Perspective. IWMI Research Report 133. Sri Lanka: Colombo.

Flörke, M., E. Kynast, I. Bärlund, S. Eisner, F. Wimmer, and J. Alcamo. 2013. Domestic and Industrial Water Uses of the Past 60 Years as a Mirror of Socio-Economic Development: A Global Simulation Study. *Global Environmental Change* 23: 144–156.

Food and Agricultural Organization of the United Nations (FAO). n.d. GeoNetwork website (accessed on 15 Feb 2015).

———. 2015. AQUASTAT website (accessed on 22 Jun 2015).

Gerbens-Leenes, P.W., A.Y. Hoekstra, and T.H. Meer. 2008. Water Footprint of Bio-Energy and Other Primary Energy Carriers. Research Report Series No. 29. Delft, Netherlands: UNESCO-IHE Institute for Water Education.

Global Expanded Water Monitoring Initiative (GEMI). 2015. Monitoring Waste Water, Water Quality and Water Resources Management: Options for Indicators and Monitoring Mechanisms for the Post-2015 Period. Paper presented at the GEMI 1st stakeholders consultation, Geneva.

Global Water Intelligence (GWI). 2014. Global Water Market 2015: Meeting the World's Water and Wastewater Needs until 2018. Oxford, UK.

Grey, D., and C.W. Sadoff. 2007. Sink or Swim? Water Security for Growth and Development. *Water Policy* 9: 545–571.

Harris, I., P.D. Jones, T.J. Osborn, and D.H. Lister. 2014. Updated High-Resolution Grids of Monthly Climatic Observations: the CRU TS3. 10 Dataset. *International Journal of Climatology* 34(3): 623–642.

Hoekstra, A.Y., and M.M. Mekonnen. 2012. The Water Footprint of Humanity. *Proceedings of the National Academy of Sciences* 109(9): 3232–3237.

Hsu, A., et al. 2014. *The 2014 Environmental Performance Index*. New Haven, CT: Yale Center for Environmental Law & Policy.

Institute for Sustainable Futures (ISF). 2014. Mozambique Water, Sanitation and Hygiene Sector Brief: prepared for AusAID by the ISF, University of Technology Sydney, Australia.

Intergovernmental Panel on Climate Change (IPCC). 2012. *Renewable Energy Sources and Climate Change Mitigation: Special Report of the Intergovernmental Panel on Climate Change.* Cambridge, UK: Cambridge University Press.

International Benchmarking Network for Water and Sanitation Utilities (IBNET). 2015. Database for Water and Sanitation Utilities. http://database.ib-net.org/Default.aspx

International Energy Agency (IEA). 2012. Water for Energy: Is Energy Becoming a Thirstier Resource? Excerpt from the *World Energy Outlook 2012.* http://www.worldenergyoutlook.org/media/weowebsite/2012/WEO_2012_Water_Excerpt.pdf (accessed on 7 Feb 2015).

———. 2015. Statistics. http://www.iea.org/statistics/statisticssearch/ (accessed on 24 Jun 2015).

International Institute for Applied Systems Analysis and Food and Agriculture Organization of the United Nations (IIASA and FAO). n.d. Global Agro-Ecological Zones. http://www.gaez.iiasa.ac.at/ (accessed on 24 Jun 2015).

International Water Center (IWC). 2015a. Final Report Key Dimension 3 (Urban Water Security) for AWDO 2016. Brisbane, Australia.

———. 2015b. Final Report Key Dimension 4 (Environmental Water Security) for AWDO 2016. Brisbane, Australia.

International Water Management Institute (IWMI). 2015. Final Report Key Dimension 2 (Economic Water Security) for AWDO 2016. Colombo, Sri Lanka.

Joint Monitoring Programme (JMP). 2015. WHO/UNICEF Joint Monitoring Programme for Water Supply and Sanitation: Data and Estimates. http://www.wssinfo.org/data-estimates/tables/ (retrieved on 26 Oct 2015).

Mahindru, S.N. 2004. *Potable Water*. New Delhi: Chaman Enterprises.

Mekonnen, M.M., P.W. Gerbens-Leenes, and A.Y. Hoekstra. 2015. The Consumptive Water Footprint of Electricity and Heat: A Global Assessment. *Environmental Science: Water Research & Technology* 1(3): 285–297.

MODIS Global Evapotranspiration Project (MOD16). n.d. The University of Montana – Numerical Terradynamyc Simulation Group. http://www.ntsg.umt.edu/project/mod16 (accessed on 15 Feb 2015).

Musinguzi, F. 2015. *Performance Measurement, Governance and Accountability*. East Africa: Water Aid.

New, M., D. Lister, M. Hulme, and I. Makin. 2002. A High-Resolution Data Set of Surface Climate over Global Land Areas. *Climate Research* 21(1): 1–25.

Nordhaus, W.D., Q. Azam, D. Corderi, K. Hood, N.M. Victor, M. Mohammed, A. Miltner, and J. Weiss2006. The G-Econ Database on Gridded Output: Methods and Data. Yale University.

Peterson, E.E., D.M. Theobald, and J.M. Ver Hoef. 2007. Geostatistical Modelling on Stream Networks: Developing Valid Covariance Matrices Based on Hydrologic Distance and Stream Flow. *Freshwater Biology* 52: 267–279.

Richter, B.D., M.M. Davis, C. Apse, and C. Konrad. 2012. A Presumptive Standard for Environmental Flow Protection. *River Research and Applications* 28: 1312-1321.

Sadoff, C.W., J.W. Hall, D. Grey, J.C.J.H. Aerts, M. Ait-Kadi, C. Brown, A. Cox, S. Dadson, D. Garrick, J. Kelman, P. McCornick, C. Ringler, M. Rosegrant, D. Whittington, and D. Wiberg. 2015. *Securing Water, Sustaining Growth: Report of the GWP/OECD Task Force on Water Security and Sustainable Growth*. Oxford, UK: University of Oxford.

Stewart-Koster, B., and S.E. Bunn. 2016. The Ecology of Water Security. In *Handbook on Water Security*, edited by C. Pahl-Wostl, A. Bhaduri, and J. Gupta. Cheltenham, UK: Edward Elgar.

United Nations (UN). 2005. Demographic Yearbook 2005. New York.

———. 2015. Millennium Development Goals Indicators. http://unstats.un.org/unsd/mdg/Data.aspx

United Nations Human Settlements Programme (UN-Habitat). 2013. Asian Sanitation Data Book 2013. Nairobi, Kenya.

United Nations University (UNU). 2013. *Water Security and the Global Water Agenda: A UN-Water Analytical Brief*. Ontario: United Nations Institute for Water, Environment and Health.

United Nations World Water Assessment Programme (WWAP). 2014. *The United Nations World Water Development Report 2014: Water and Energy*. Paris: UNESCO.

United States Energy Information Administration (USEIA). n.d. International Energy Statistics. http://www.eia.gov/countries/ (accessed on 15 Jun 2015).

van Beek, E., and W. Lincklaen Arriens. 2014. Water Security: Putting the Concept into Practise. TEC Background Paper No. 20. Stockholm: Global Water Partnership Technical Committee.

Vörösmarty, C., C.A. Federer, and A.L. Schloss. 1998. Potential Evaporation Functions Compared on US Watersheds: Possible Implications for Global-Scale Water Balance and Terrestrial Ecosystem Modeling. *Journal of Hydrology* 207(3-4): 147–169.

Vörösmarty, C. J., P.B. McIntyre, M.O. Gessner, D. Dudgeon, P. Green, S. Glidden, S.E. Bunn, C.A. Sullivan, C. Reidy Liermann, and P.M. Davies. 2010. Global Threats to Human Water Security and River Biodiversity. *Nature* 467: 555–561.

Warszawski, L., K. Frieler, V. Huber, F. Piontek, O. Serdeczny, and J. Schewe. 2013. The Inter-Sectoral Impact Model Intercomparison Project (ISI–MIP): Project framework, PNAS 2014 111 (9) 3228-3232 (published ahead of print 16 Dec 2013) doi:10.1073/pnas.1312330110

Wisser, D., B.M. Fekete, C.J. Vörösmarty, and A.H. Schumann. 2010. Reconstructing 20th Century Global Hydrography: A Contribution to the Global Terrestrial Network- Hydrology (GTN-H). Hydrol. *Earth Sys. Sci.* 14: 1-24.

World Bank. 2015a. World Bank Open Data. http://data.worldbank.org/

————. 2015b. World Development Indicators. data.worldbank.org/products/wdi (accessed on 15 Oct 2015).

World Health Organization (WHO). 2013. WHO Methods and Data Sources for Global Burden of Disease Estimates 2000–2011. Global Health Estimates Technical Paper WHO/HIS/HSI/GHE/2013.4. p. 5.

World Health Organization and United Nations Children's Fund (WHO and UNICEF). 2000. *Global Water Supply and Sanitation Assessment 2000 Report*. Geneva and New York, NY.

Appendixes

APPENDIX 1

Population and Land Area Statistics of the Asian Water Development Outlook Economies in 2014

Table A1.1: Population and Land Area Statistics, by Economy

Region	Economy	National Population (2014)		Urban Population (2014)		Urban Growth (2014)	Land Area
		x1000	growth %	x1000	%	%	Sq. Km.
CWA	Afghanistan	31,281	2.9	8,221	26	4.0	652,860
CWA	Armenia	2,984	0.4	1,874	63	0.0	28,470
ADV	Australia	23,630	1.5	21,099	89	1.4	7,682,300
CWA	Azerbaijan	9,515	1.3	5,172	54	1.6	82,659
SA	Bangladesh	158,513	1.2	53,127	34	3.6	130,170
SA	Bhutan	766	1.3	290	38	3.6	38,117
ADV	Brunei Darussalam	423	1.4	325	77	1.7	5,270
SEA	Cambodia	15,408	1.6	3,165	21	2.8	176,520
EA	China, People's Republic of	1,393,784	0.5	758,360	54	2.9	9,388,211
PA	Cook Islands	21	0.5	15	74	0.8	240
PA	Fiji	887	0.7	473	53	1.4	18,270
CWA	Georgia	4,323	–1.0	2,311	53	–0.1	69,490
ADV	Hong Kong, China	7,260	0.9	7,260	100	0.8	1,050
SA	India	1,267,402	1.2	410,204	32	2.4	2,973,190
SEA	Indonesia	252,812	1.2	133,983	53	2.6	1,811,570
ADV	Japan	127,000	–0.2	118,136	93	0.5	364,560
CWA	Kazakhstan	16,607	1.5	8,850	53	0.9	2,699,700
PA	Kiribati	104	1.8	46	44	1.8	810
ADV	Korea, Republic of	49,512	0.4	40,778	82	0.6	97,466
CWA	Kyrgyz Republic	5,625	1.7	2,002	36	1.7	191,800
SEA	Lao People's Democratic Republic	6,894	1.7	2,589	38	4.9	230,800
SEA	Malaysia	30,188	1.4	22,342	74	2.6	328,550
SA	Maldives	352	1.8	156	44	4.4	300
PA	Marshall Islands	58	0.2	42	73	0.6	180
PA	Micronesia, Federated States of	104	0.4	23	22	0.5	700
EA	Mongolia	2,881	1.7	2,052	71	2.7	1,553,560
SEA	Myanmar	53,719	0.9	18,023	34	2.5	653,080

continued on next page

Table *continued*

Region	Economy	National Population (2014)		Urban Population (2014)		Urban Growth (2014)	Land Area
		x1000	growth %	x1000	%	%	Sq. Km.
PA	Nauru	11	0.2	11	100	0.3	20
SA	Nepal	28,121	1.2	5,130	18	3.2	143,350
ADV	New Zealand	4,551	0.7	3,926	86	1.0	263,310
CWA	Pakistan	185,133	2.1	70,912	38	2.8	770,880
PA	Palau	21	0.8	18	86	1.6	460
PA	Papua New Guinea	476	2.1	971	13	2.2	452,860
SEA	Philippines	100,096	1.6	44,531	44	1.4	298,170
PA	Samoa	192	0.7	37	19	-0.2	2,830
ADV	Singapore	5,517	1.8	5,517	100	1.9	707
PA	Solomon Islands	573	2.0	125	22	4.2	27,990
SA	Sri Lanka	21,446	0.5	3,929	18	0.9	62,710
EA	Taipei,China	23,434	0.2	23,434			
CWA	Tajikistan	8,409	2.2	2,245	27	2.7	139,960
SEA	Thailand	67,223	0.4	33,056	49	2.9	510,890
PA	Timor-Leste	1,152	2.4	370	32	3.8	14,870
PA	Tonga	106	0.5	25	24	0.7	720
CWA	Turkmenistan	5,307	1.3	2,637	50	2.0	469,930
PA	Tuvalu	10	0.2	5	52	1.9	30
CWA	Uzbekistan	29,325	1.5	10,638	36	1.5	425,400
PA	Vanuatu	258	2.2	67	26	3.4	12,190
SEA	Viet Nam	92,548	1.1	30,503	33	3.0	310,070

Sq. Km. = square kilometer.

Sources: National population and urban population from WHO-UNICEF JMP database (http://www.wssinfo.org/satra-estimates/tables/); Population growth: UNESCAP database; Land area: World Bank World Development Indicators database.

Table A1.2: Population and Land Area Statistics, by Region

Region	Economy	National Population (2014) x1000	Growth Rate %	Urban Population (2014) x1000	%	Urban Growth (2014) %	Land Area Sq. Km.
ADV	Australia	23,630	1.5	21,099	89	1.4	7,682,300
ADV	Brunei Darussalam	423	1.4	325	77	1.7	5,270
ADV	Hong Kong, China	7,260	0.9	7,260	100	0.8	1,050
ADV	Japan	127,000	−0.2	118,136	93	0.5	364,560
ADV	Korea, Republic of	49,512	0.4	40,778	82	0.6	97,466
ADV	New Zealand	4,551	0.7	3,926	86	1.0	263,310
ADV	Singapore	5,517	1.8	5,517	100	1.9	707
	Region Adv. Economies	**217,893**	**0.2**	**197,041**	**90**		**8,414,663**
CWA	Afghanistan	31,281	2.9	8,221	26	4.0	652,860
CWA	Armenia	2,984	0.4	1,874	63	0.0	28,470
CWA	Azerbaijan	9,515	1.3	5,172	54	1.6	82,659
CWA	Georgia	4,323	−1.0	2,311	53	−0.1	69,490
CWA	Kazakhstan	16,607	1.5	8,850	53	0.9	2,699,700
CWA	Kyrgyz Republic	5,625	1.7	2,002	36	1.7	191,800
CWA	Pakistan	185,133	2.1	70,912	38	2.8	770,880
CWA	Tajikistan	8,409	2.2	2,245	27	2.7	139,960
CWA	Turkmenistan	5,307	1.3	2,637	50	2.0	469,930
CWA	Uzbekistan	29,325	1.5	10,638	36	1.5	425,400
	Region Central and West Asia	**298,508**	**2.0**	**114,862**	**38**		**5,531,149**
EA	China, People's Republic of	1,393,784	0.5	758,360	54	2.9	9,388,211
EA	Mongolia	2,881	1.7	2,052	71	2.7	1,553,560
EA	Taipei,China	23,434	0.2		0		
	Region East Asia	**1,420,099**	**0.5**	**760,412**	**54**		**10,941,771**
PA	Cook Islands	21	0.5	15	74	0.8	240
PA	Fiji	887	0.7	473	53	1.4	18,270
PA	Kiribati	104	1.8	46	44	1.8	810
PA	Marshall Islands	58	0.2	42	73	0.6	180
PA	Micronesia, Fed. States of	104	0.4	23	22	0.5	700
PA	Nauru	11	0.2	11	100	0.3	20
PA	Palau	21	0.8	18	86	1.6	460
PA	Papua New Guinea	7,476	2.1	971	13	2.2	452,860
PA	Samoa	192	0.7	37	19	−0.2	2,830
PA	Solomon Islands	573	2.0	125	22	4.2	27,990
PA	Timor-Leste	1,152	2.4	370	32	3.8	14,870
PA	Tonga	106	0.5	25	24	0.7	720

continued on next page

Table *continued*

Region	Economy	National Population (2014) x1000	Growth Rate %	Urban Population (2014) x1000	%	Urban Growth (2014) %	Land Area Sq. Km.
PA	Tuvalu	10	0.2	5	52	1.9	30
PA	Vanuatu	258	2.2	67	26	3.4	12,190
	Region Pacific	**10,972**	**1.9**	**2,229**	**20**		**532,170**
SA	Bangladesh	158,513	1.2	53,127	34	3.6	130,170
SA	Bhutan	766	1.3	290	38	3.6	38,117
SA	India	1,267,402	1.2	410,204	32	2.4	2,973,190
SA	Maldives	352	1.8	156	44	4.4	300
SA	Nepal	28,121	1.2	5,130	18	3.2	143,350
SA	Sri Lanka	21,446	0.5	3,929	18	0.9	62,710
	Region South Asia	**1,476,598**	**1.2**	**472,836**	**32**		**3,347,837**
SEA	Cambodia	15,408	1.6	3,165	21	2.8	176,520
SEA	Indonesia	252,812	1.2	133,983	53	2.6	1,811,570
SEA	Lao People's Democratic Republic	6,894	1.7	2,589	38	4.9	230,800
SEA	Malaysia	30,188	1.4	22,342	74	2.6	328,550
SEA	Myanmar	53,719	0.9	18,023	34	2.5	653,080
SEA	Philippines	100,096	1.6	44,531	44	1.4	298,170
SEA	Thailand	67,223	0.4	33,056	49	2.9	510,890
SEA	Viet Nam	92,548	1.1	30,503	33	3.0	310,070
	Region Southeast Asia	**618,889**	**1.2**	**288,192**	**47**		**4,319,650**

ADV = Advanced Economies, CWA = Central and West Asia region, EA = East Asia region, PA = Pacific region, SA = South Asia region, SEA = Southeast Asia region, Sq. Km. = square kilometer.
Sources: National population and urban population from WHO-UNICEF JMP database (http://www.wssinfo.org/satra-estimates/tables/); Population growth: UNESCAP database; Land area: World Bank World Development Indicators database.

APPENDIX 2
Methodological Approach for Small Island States

The methodological approach followed for the Asian Water Development Outlook (AWDO) appears to be less suitable for small countries, i.e. countries smaller than 10–20,000 square kilometers, typically the small island states. In particular, economic water security (KD2) and environmental water security (KD4) are difficult or impossible to apply in these small areas. Data availability is another issue for most of the small countries. The Pacific region (with the exception of Papua New Guinea) consists

completely of small countries. Other small economies are Brunei Darussalam; Hong Kong, China; the Maldives; and Singapore. Table A2.1 provides an overview of the small economies.

Brunei Darussalam; Hong Kong, China; and Singapore are advanced economies. The other countries, including the Maldives from the South Asia region, can indeed be labeled as small island states.

Table A2.1: Overview of Data on Small Economies

Region	Economy	National Population (2014) x1000	Growth Rate %	Urban Population (2014) x1000	%	Urban Growth (2014) %	Land Area Sq. Km.
ADV	Brunei Darussalam	423	1.4	325	77	1.7	5,270
PA	Cook Islands	21	0.5	15	74	0.8	240
PA	Fiji	887	0.7	473	53	1.4	18,270
ADV	Hong Kong, China	7,260	0.9	7,260	100	0.8	1,050
PA	Kiribati	104	1.8	46	44	1.8	810
SA	Maldives	352	1.8	156	44	4.4	300
PA	Marshall Islands	58	0.2	42	73	0.6	180
PA	Micronesia, Fed. States of	104	0.4	23	22	0.5	700
PA	Nauru	11	0.2	11	100	0.3	20
PA	Palau	21	0.8	18	86	1.6	460
PA	Samoa	192	0.7	37	19	−0.2	2,830
ADV	Singapore	5,517	1.8	5,517	100	1.9	707
PA	Solomon Islands	573	2	125	22	4.2	27,990
PA	Timor-Leste	1,152	2.4	370	32	3.8	14,870
PA	Tonga	106	0.5	25	24	0.7	720
PA	Tuvalu	10	0.2	5	52	1.9	30
PA	Vanuatu	258	2.2	67	26	3.4	12,190

Sq. Km. = square kilometer.
Source: ADB.

Given the lack of data and the nonapplicability of the methodology, we used an expert opinion approach as an additional source of information to determine the scores for the key dimensions. The experts were asked to score the following indicators on a scale of 1–5:

Household water security (KD1)

- % piped water supply*
- % sanitation*
- Disability-affected life year (DALY) score

Economic water security (KD2)

- Constraints to use water for economic activities

Urban water security (KD3)

- % urban water supply*
- % urban waste water*
- urban drainage

Environmental water security (KD4)

- Water quality

Resilience to water-related disasters (KD5)

- Floods and storms
- Drought
- Storm surges

The scoring of these indicators follow the linear scoring approach of AWDO (1 = bad, 5 = excellent) with the exception of the piped water and access to safe sanitation indicators (indicated with a * in list), for which the following scoring is applied:

Table A2.2: Scoring Table for Piped Water Supply and Sanitation

Access (%)	Score
< 60	1
60–70	2
70–80	3
80–90	4
≥ 90	5

Source: ADB.

The consulted experts are

- Pacific islands: Stephen Blaik, Principal Urban Development Specialist, Asian Development Bank
- Brunei Darussalam; Hong Kong, China; Maldives; and Singapore: AWDO 2016 team

The expert opinion on the Pacific Islands is given in Table A2.2. The expert opinions on the other small countries are described, where needed because of missing of data, in the chapters on the key dimensions.

The scores are used for the results tables of the five key dimensions. How this is done is described in the chapters on the key dimensions. In cases in which reliable data were available, the data were used and not expert opinion. In some cases, a combination of data and expert opinion was used.

Table A2.3: Result of Expert Judgment of Pacific Small Island States

Economy	KD1 (WASH)			KD2 (Econ.)	KD3 (Urban)			KD4 (Env.)	KD5 (Resilience)		
	% Piped Water	% Sanitation	Hygiene (DALY)	General Conditions	Urban Water	Urban Waste	Urban Drainage	Env. (Water)	Floods/ Storms	Drought	Storm Surges
Cook Islands	5	5	4	3	5	5	5	4	3	4	2
Fiji	4	4	4	5	5	5	4	3	2	4	4
Kiribati	1	1	1	1	4	2	2	1	1	2	1
Marshall Islands	3	3	1	1	4	3	2	3	2	2	1
Micronesia, Fed. States of	1	3	3	4	4	4	4	4	2	3	3
Nauru	4	4	4	3	5	5	5	5	4	4	5
Palau	5	5	4	3	5	5	5	4	4	2	3
Samoa	4	4	3	4	5	5	4	4	2	4	4
Solomon Islands	1	1	1	3	3	1	3	4	2	4	4
Timor-Leste	1	1	1	3	3	2	3	3	3	4	4
Tonga	4	4	4	4	5	4	4	2	1	4	1
Tuvalu	3	3	3	1	5	5	4	4	1	2	1
Vanuatu	1	1	2	4	3	2	2	3	1	4	4

DALY = disability-adjusted life year, KD = key dimension.
Source: ADB.

Results of the Asian Water Development Outlook 2016 and Comparison with the Asian Water Development Outlook 2013

This appendix describes the detailed results for all key dimensions and the National Water Security Index (NWSI) for three cases of the Asian Water Development Outlook (AWDO):

- AWDO 2013 as published;
- AWDO 2013 adjusted: applying the (new) AWDO 2016 methodology on AWDO 2013 data; and
- AWDO 2016: the final results that are included in the AWDO 2016 report.

The presentation of the results for these three cases in one overview enables us to draw conclusions on

- the consequences of the application of the new AWDO 2016 methodology, by comparing AWDO 2103 as published with AWDO 2013 adjusted; and
- the progress the countries have been making to increase water security, by comparing AWDO 2016 with AWDO 2013 adjusted.

The comparison between the three cases will be done at two levels. The *first level* is to carry out the comparisons of the key dimensions (KDs) for the three cases based on the calculated scores with the maxima of 15 for KD1, 20 for KD2, 16 for KD3, 15 for KD4, and 15 for KD5. The KD indices (1–5 scale) will not be used in this comparison because the bandings for the key dimensions and the NWSI have been changed in AWDO 2016. In cases of major differences in results, comments and explanations are given on these differences. This is described in sections 1–5 for the five key dimensions.

The *second level* is the comparison based on the 20-scale scores for the key dimensions and the 100-scale for the NWSI. Having the key dimensions now at a same level enables a more consistent comparison. This will be described for the key dimensions and the NWSI together in section 6.

Finally, section 7 gives a summary assessment of the changes in the methodology and the progress the countries have been making in improving their national water security between the publication of AWDO 2013 and AWDO 2016.

Please note that this appendix is based on the detailed key dimension reports prepared for AWDO 2016. For additional information, refer to these reports.

1 Results and Comparison for Household Water Security

Table A3.1 presents the detailed results for KD1 for the three cases expressed in terms of scores on a 1–15 scale. The coloring of the scores indicates how missing data have been dealt with. This is explained in the main text of this methodology report.

The differences in scores between the three cases are given in the three rightmost columns. The coloring in these columns indicates the direction and size of the difference: green for higher scores and red for lower scores. Next to the rightmost column are indicators for remarks made by the AWDO team on these differences:

a) More consistent (possibly better) estimates are now available from JMP (2015). The data used in AWDO 2013 were overestimated.

Table A3.1: Detailed Results for Household Water Security (KD1)

#	Economy	AWDO 2013 (published) PW Index	San Index	DALY Index	KD1 Score	KD1 Index 2010	AWDO 2013 adjusted PW Index	San Index	DALY Index	KD1 Score	KD1 Index 2010	AWDO 2016 PW Index	San Index	DALY Index	KD1 Score	KD1 Index 2014	KD1 scores 2013pub	2013 adj	2016	Differences 2013adj-2013pub	2016-2013adj	2016-2013pub	Remarks
1	Afghanistan	1	1	1	3	1	1	1	1	3	1	1	1	1	3	3	3	3	3	0	0	0	
2	Armenia	5	5	3	13	4	5	4	3	12	4	5	4	5	14	5	13	12	14	-1	2	1	
3	Australia	5	5	5	15	5	5	5	5	15	5	5	5	5	15	5	15	15	15	0	0	0	b,d
4	Azerbaijan	1	4	1	6	2	1	4	1	6	2	2	4	3	9	3	6	6	9	0	3	3	
5	Bangladesh	1	1	1	3	1	1	1	1	3	1	1	1	1	3	2	3	3	3	0	0	0	
6	Bhutan	1	1	1	3	1	1	1	1	3	1	1	1	3	5	2	3	3	5	0	2	2	
7	Brunei Darussalam	5	4	5	14	5	5	5	5	15	5	5	5	5	15	5	14	15	15	1	0	1	
8	Cambodia	1	1	1	3	1	1	1	1	3	1	1	3	1	5	2	3	3	5	0	2	2	
9	China, People's Republic of	2	2	3	7	3	2	3	3	8	3	3	3	5	11	4	7	8	11	1	3	4	d,e
10	Cook Islands	5	5	4	14	5	4	5	3	12	4	3	5	4	12	4	14	12	12	-2	0	-2	a
11	Fiji	4	4	4	12	3	3	4	3	10	3	2	5	4	11	4	12	10	11	-2	1	-1	
12	Georgia	3	5	2	10	3	2	5	2	9	3	3	4	5	12	4	10	9	12	-1	3	2	d
13	Hong Kong, China	4	5	4	13	4	5	5	4	14	5	5	5	4	14	5	13	14	14	1	0	1	
14	India	1	1	1	3	1	1	1	1	3	1	1	1	1	3	2	3	3	3	0	0	0	
15	Indonesia	1	1	1	3	1	1	3	1	5	2	1	2	3	6	2	3	5	6	2	1	3	
16	Japan	5	5	5	15	5	5	5	5	15	5	5	5	5	15	5	15	15	15	0	0	0	d
17	Kazakhstan	2	5	1	7	3	2	5	1	8	3	2	5	4	11	4	7	8	11	1	3	4	d
18	Kiribati	1	1	1	3	1	1	1	1	3	1	1	1	1	3	2	3	3	3	0	0	0	
19	Korea, Republic of	5	5	4	14	5	5	5	4	14	5	5	5	5	15	5	14	14	15	0	1	1	
20	Kyrgyz Republic	2	4	1	7	3	2	4	1	7	2	2	4	4	10	3	7	7	10	0	3	3	d
21	Lao People's Democratic Republic	1	2	1	4	2	1	1	1	3	1	1	3	1	5	2	4	3	5	-1	2	1	
22	Malaysia	5	5	4	14	5	5	5	4	14	5	5	5	5	15	5	14	14	15	0	1	1	d
23	Maldives	1	5	2	8	3	1	5	2	8	3	1	5	4	11	4	8	8	11	0	3	3	
24	Marshall Islands	3	3	2	6	2	3	3	2	6	2	1	3	1	5	2	6	6	5	0	-1	-1	
25	Micronesia, Federated States of	5	1	3	9	3	1	1	3	5	2	1	1	3	5	2	9	5	5	-4	0	-4	c
26	Mongolia	1	1	1	3	1	1	1	1	3	1	1	1	3	5	2	3	3	5	0	2	2	
27	Myanmar	1	3	1	5	2	1	3	1	5	2	1	3	2	6	2	5	5	6	0	1	1	
28	Nauru	1	2	3	6	3	2	2	3	7	3	2	2	4	8	2	6	7	8	1	1	2	
29	Nepal	1	1	1	3	1	1	1	1	3	1	1	1	2	4	2	3	3	4	0	1	1	
30	New Zealand	5	5	5	15	5	5	5	5	15	5	5	5	5	15	5	15	15	15	0	0	0	
31	Pakistan	1	1	1	3	1	1	1	1	3	1	1	2	1	4	2	3	3	4	0	1	1	
32	Palau	1	5	3	9	3	5	5	3	13	4	5	5	4	14	4	9	13	14	4	1	5	
33	Papua New Guinea	1	3	2	6	2	1	1	1	3	1	1	1	1	3	2	6	3	3	-3	0	-3	
34	Philippines	1	3	2	6	2	1	3	2	6	2	1	3	3	7	2	6	6	7	0	1	1	
35	Samoa	4	5	3	12	4	4	5	3	12	4	4	5	3	12	4	12	12	12	0	0	0	
36	Singapore	5	5	5	15	5	5	5	5	15	5	5	5	5	15	5	15	15	15	0	0	0	
37	Solomon Islands	1	3	1	5	2	1	3	1	5	2	1	1	2	4	1	5	5	4	0	-1	-1	
38	Sri Lanka	1	5	4	10	3	1	5	4	10	3	1	5	4	10	3	10	10	10	0	0	0	
39	Taipei,China	5	2	4	11	4	5	4	1	10	3	5	2	4	11	4	11	10	11	-1	1	0	f
40	Tajikistan	1	5	1	7	3	1	5	1	7	2	1	5	1	7	2	7	7	7	0	0	0	
41	Thailand	1	5	2	8	3	1	5	2	8	3	3	5	2	10	3	8	8	10	0	2	2	
42	Timor-Leste	1	2	1	4	2	1	2	1	4	1	1	1	1	3	1	4	4	3	0	-1	-1	
43	Tonga	4	5	2	11	4	3	5	3	11	4	3	5	4	12	3	11	11	12	0	1	1	
44	Turkmenistan	3	2	1	6	2	1	5	1	7	2	1	5	3	9	3	6	7	9	1	2	3	c
45	Tuvalu	5	4	2	11	4	5	4	2	11	4	5	4	3	12	4	11	11	12	0	1	1	
46	Uzbekistan	1	5	1	7	3	1	5	1	7	3	1	5	3	9	3	7	7	9	0	2	2	
47	Vanuatu	1	1	3	5	2	1	1	3	5	2	1	1	2	4	3	5	5	4	0	-1	-1	
48	Viet Nam	1	3	3	7	3	1	2	3	6	2	1	2	4	8	3	7	6	8	-1	2	1	c
					427					427					427		384	380	427	-4	47	43	

sum		-4	47	43	
pos.		10	51	54	
neg.		-14	-4	-11	
		-1.0%	12.4%	11.2%	
		2.6%	13.4%	14.1%	
		-3.6%	-1.1%	-2.9%	

No regular data available – use has been made of other resources

no data available – we used the score of 2013

EO used (Pacific)

"Own" EO

Source: ADB.

b) More consistent (possibly better) estimates are now available from JMP (2015). The data used in AWDO 2013 were underestimated.
c) Data are now available from JMP (2015). Expert judgment of the missing data in AWDO 2013 was not accurate.
d) Due to a significant decrease in disability-adjusted life years (DALYs).
e) Noticeable increase in access to piped water and improved sanitation.
f) Slight difference from our calculation because the access rate of improved sanitation (69.87%) was rounded up to 70%, thus the sanitation index was 3 rather than 2.

The adjustment in methodology to determine KD1 has been minor. See the main text on KD1 for a description of this adjustment.

The following conclusions were drawn from the results for KD1:

- The impact of the (slightly) changed methodology is limited.
- The difference between AWDO 2016 and AWDO 2013 is in the order of 10%. Most of this increase is due to improved performance on this key dimension.
- Some of the difference is due to over- and underestimation of the AWDO 2013 scores based on expert judgment.

2 Results and Comparison for Economic Water Security (KD2)

Table A3.2 presents the detailed results for KD2 for the three cases expressed in terms of scores on a 1–20 scale. The coloring of the scores indicates how missing data have been dealt with. This is explained in the main text of this Methodology report.

The differences in scores between the three cases are given in the three rightmost columns. The coloring in these columns indicates the direction and size of the difference: green for higher scores and red for lower scores. Next to the rightmost

column are indicators for remarks made by the AWDO team on these differences:

a) This may have been an underestimate using the previous approach.
b) Better data availability likely explains the change.
c) Better data availability explains the change; the new approach yielded results in all four components, as opposed to just one component using the previous approach.
d) Data constraints may affect the results.
e) This may have been an underestimate using the previous approach; the updated scoring is likely more accurate.
f) This may have been an overestimate using the previous approach; the updated scoring is likely more accurate.

An additional remark by the KD team is the following:

- We looked at the nine economies whose scores increased by more than 5 between AWDO 2013 (published) and AWDO 2016. The scores for certain countries such as Australia and Singapore were likely too low in AWDO 2013; the new scoring is likely more accurate. Scores for other countries such as Brunei Darussalam and the Maldives were likely affected by limited data last time; more data have now been used to populate the indicators, so the scores for these countries are likely stronger. Vanuatu may be considered in a similar way to Brunei Darussalam and the Maldives. The four remaining countries are Pacific island countries with data constraints. Data availability for these countries improved between AWDO 2013 (published) and AWDO 2016, but their data are likely still too constrained to draw strong conclusions on explanations for improvement.

The adjustment in the methodology to determine KD2 has been major (see the main text on KD2 for a description of this adjustment).

The following conclusions were drawn from the results for KD2:

- The impact of the changed methodology is significant. Some countries score considerably higher (by up to 10 points on a 20-point scale); other countries score considerably lower (by up to –6 points). Analyzing those changes, we conclude that the new approach provides better results.
- The differences between AWDO 2016 and AWDO 2013 (adjusted) are in the order of 5% (increase).
- Data constraints are an important issue for KD2.

3   Results and Comparison for Urban Water Security (KD3)

Table A3.3 presents the detailed results for KD3 for the three cases expressed in terms of scores on a 1–16 scale. The coloring of the scores indicates how missing data have been dealt with. This is explained in the main text of this Methodology report.

The differences in scores between the three cases are given in the three rightmost columns. The coloring in these columns indicates the direction and size of the difference: green for higher scores and red for lower scores. Next to the rightmost column are indicators for remarks made by the AWDO team on these differences:

a) Bangladesh: High economic growth of 6% leads to reduced drainage losses.
b) Change in urbanization rate
c) Change in wastewater collection: now empirical data
d) River health improvement
e) Increased drainage damage
f) Improved water supply

The adjustment in the methodology to determine KD3 has been limited (see the main text on KD3 for a description of this adjustment).

The following conclusions were drawn from the results for KD3:

- The impact of the changed methodology is about 10%.
- AWDO 2016 scores are slightly (2%) lower compared with AWDO 2013 (adjusted) scores. This might be due to the growing urbanization in the region but also due to new data.

4   Results and Comparison for Environmental Water Security (KD4)

Table A3.4 presents the detailed results for KD4 for the three cases expressed in terms of scores on a 1–15 scale. The coloring of the scores indicates how missing data have been dealt with. This is explained in the main text of this methodology report. The main "missing data" are for the small island states. These are not actually missing but could not be calculated because the methodology for KD4 could not be applied in these cases. Expert estimates have been used to determine the scores. These estimates enabled these small island states (to some extent) to be comparable to the other countries.

It should be noted that the adjusted 2013 case only includes the updated methodology for the river health index (RHI). It does not include the flow and governance subindicators that were added to KD4 later in the preparation phase of AWDO 2016.

The differences in scores between the three cases are given in the three rightmost columns. The coloring in these columns indicates the direction and size of the difference: green for higher scores and red for lower scores.

The adjustment in the methodology to determine KD4 has been major (see the main text on KD1 for a description of this adjustment).

Table A3.2: Detailed Results for Economic Water Security (KD2)

#	Economy	AWDO 2013 (published)						AWDO 2013 adjusted						AWDO 2016							KD2 scores			Differences			Remarks
		Agriculture	Industry	Energy	TOTAL 30pt	TOTAL est. 30pt	TOTAL est. 20pt	Broad Econ	Agriculture	Industry	Energy	KD2 score	Adjusted KD2 score	Broad Econ	Agriculture	Industry	Energy	KD2 score	Adjusted KD2 score	KD2 Index	2013pub	2013 adj	2016	2013adj–2013pub	2016–2013adj	2016–2013pub	
1	Afghanistan	5.22	–	–	–	9.00	6.00	2.13	1.00	4.00	1.00	8.13	8.13	2.1	1.0	4.0	1.0	8.1	8.1	3	6.00	8.13	8.13	2.1	0.0	2.1	
2	Armenia	6.56	5.56	7.11	19.22	19.22	12.81	3.06	2.00	4.00	2.00	11.06	11.06	3.1	3.0	4.0	3.0	13.1	13.1	3	12.81	11.06	13.06	-1.8	2.0	0.2	
3	Australia	5.89	5.56	5.78	17.22	17.22	11.48	4.06	3.00	5.00	4.50	16.56	16.56	4.1	3.0	5.0	4.5	16.6	16.6	3	11.48	16.56	16.56	5.1	0.0	5.1	a
4	Azerbaijan	5.56	5.56	7.78	18.89	18.89	12.59	3.69	2.50	3.00	3.50	12.69	12.69	3.7	2.5	3.0	3.0	12.2	12.2	3	12.59	12.69	12.19	0.1	-0.5	-0.4	
5	Bangladesh	4.89	5.56	3.78	14.22	14.22	9.48	3.06	2.00	4.00	3.00	12.06	12.06	3.1	3.0	5.0	3.0	14.1	14.1	3	9.48	12.06	14.06	2.6	2.0	4.6	
6	Bhutan	4.67	4.67	7.33	16.67	16.67	11.11	3.17	1.00	5.00	5.00	14.17	14.17	3.2	3.0	5.0	3.0	14.2	14.2	3	11.11	14.17	14.17	3.1	0.0	3.1	
7	Brunei Darussalam	–	–	4.44	–	9.00	6.00	3.19	2.50	ND	5.00	10.69	14.25	3.2	2.5	ND	5.0	10.7	14.3	3	6.00	14.25	14.25	8.3	0.0	8.3	b
8	Cambodia	3.56	4.22	6.44	14.22	14.22	9.48	3.17	2.50	5.00	3.00	13.67	13.67	3.2	3.0	5.0	1.5	12.7	12.7	3	9.48	13.67	12.67	4.2	-1.0	3.2	
9	China, People's Republic of	7.22	6.22	7.11	20.56	20.56	13.70	3.75	2.50	3.00	3.50	12.75	12.75	3.8	3.5	4.0	4.0	15.3	15.3	4	13.70	12.75	15.25	-1.0	2.5	1.5	
10	Cook Islands	–	–	5.56	–	9.00	6.00	1.75	ND	ND	1.00	2.75	5.50	1.8	2.0	2.0	1.0	6.8	6.8	1	6.00	5.50	6.75	-0.5	1.3	0.8	
11	Fiji	5.56	4.89	7.11	17.56	17.56	11.70	3.33	2.50	5.00	1.00	11.83	11.83	3.3	2.5	5.0	1.0	11.8	11.8	3	11.70	11.83	11.83	0.1	0.0	0.1	
12	Georgia	6.78	–	8.89	–	15.67	10.44	4.00	1.50	3.00	1.50	10.00	10.00	4.0	1.5	3.0	2.0	10.5	10.5	2	10.44	10.00	10.50	-0.4	0.5	0.1	
13	Hong Kong, China	–	–	–	–	21.00	14.00	1.00	5.00	ND	5.00	11.00	14.67	1.0	5.0	ND	5.0	11.0	14.7	3	14.00	14.67	14.67	0.7	0.0	0.7	
14	India	6.11	5.11	5.56	16.78	16.78	11.19	2.88	2.50	4.00	2.00	11.38	11.38	2.9	3.5	4.0	2.5	12.9	12.9	3	11.19	11.38	12.88	0.2	1.5	1.7	
15	Indonesia	6.89	5.56	7.11	19.56	19.56	13.04	3.31	3.00	4.00	2.50	12.81	12.81	3.3	3.0	5.0	3.0	14.3	14.3	3	13.04	12.81	14.31	-0.2	1.5	1.3	
16	Japan	7.78	6.44	6.22	20.44	20.44	13.63	3.25	1.00	5.00	4.50	13.75	13.75	3.3	1.5	5.0	4.5	14.3	14.3	3	13.63	13.75	14.25	0.1	0.5	0.6	
17	Kazakhstan	6.11	6.44	8.89	21.44	21.44	14.30	4.25	3.00	3.00	4.50	14.75	14.75	4.3	3.0	3.0	4.5	14.8	14.8	3	14.30	14.75	14.75	0.5	0.0	0.5	
18	Kiribati	–	–	3.56	–	3.50	2.33	1.50	2.50	ND	1.00	5.00	6.67	1.5	3.0	ND	1.0	5.5	7.3	2	2.33	6.67	7.33	4.3	0.7	5.0	
19	Korea, Republic of	6.67	5.33	5.33	17.33	17.33	11.56	3.13	2.50	5.00	5.00	15.63	15.63	3.1	2.5	5.0	5.0	15.6	15.6	4	11.56	15.63	15.63	4.1	0.0	4.1	
20	Kyrgyz Republic	5.56	4.22	7.11	16.89	16.89	11.26	3.81	2.50	2.00	3.00	11.31	11.31	3.8	2.5	3.0	3.0	12.3	12.3	3	11.26	11.31	12.31	0.1	1.0	1.1	
21	Lao People's Democratic Republic	5.00	4.67	8.67	18.33	18.33	12.22	3.31	2.50	3.00	1.00	9.81	9.81	3.3	3.0	3.0	2.0	11.3	11.3	3	12.22	9.81	11.31	-2.4	1.5	-0.9	
22	Malaysia	6.67	6.67	8.00	21.33	21.33	14.22	3.94	3.00	3.00	5.00	14.94	14.94	3.9	3.0	4.0	4.5	15.4	15.4	4	14.22	14.94	15.44	0.7	0.5	1.2	
23	Maldives	–	–	1.33	–	3.50	2.33	3.00	3.00	5.00	1.00	12.00	12.00	3.0	3.0	5.0	1.0	12.0	12.0	3	2.33	12.00	12.00	9.7	0.0	9.7	c
24	Marshall Islands	–	–	1.33	–	3.50	2.33	2.25	1.00	ND	ND	3.25	6.50	2.3	3.0	1.0	1.0	7.3	7.3	2	2.33	6.50	7.25	4.2	0.8	4.9	d
25	Micronesia, Federated States of	–	–	5.56	–	9.00	6.00	1.00	3.00	ND	ND	4.00	8.00	1.0	4.0	3.0	3.0	11.0	11.0	2	6.00	8.00	11.00	2.0	3.0	5.0	d
26	Mongolia	2.11	1.78	4.89	8.78	8.78	5.85	3.31	1.00	3.00	3.00	10.31	10.31	3.3	1.0	3.0	3.0	10.3	10.3	2	5.85	10.31	10.31	4.5	0.0	4.5	
27	Myanmar	4.89	4.22	8.44	17.56	17.56	11.70	3.88	2.50	5.00	1.50	12.88	12.88	3.9	3.0	5.0	1.5	13.4	13.4	3	11.70	12.88	13.38	1.2	0.5	1.7	
28	Nauru	–	–	1.33	–	3.50	2.33	1.50	ND	ND	5.00	6.50	13.00	1.5	2.0	2.0	3.0	8.5	8.5	2	2.33	13.00	8.50	10.7	-4.5	6.2	
29	Nepal	5.67	4.00	7.33	17.00	17.00	11.33	2.81	2.00	5.00	1.00	10.81	10.81	2.8	2.5	5.0	1.0	11.3	11.3	2	11.33	10.81	11.31	-0.5	0.5	0.0	
30	New Zealand	4.89	5.56	8.44	18.89	18.89	12.59	4.56	2.50	5.00	3.50	15.56	15.56	4.6	2.5	5.0	3.5	15.6	15.6	4	12.59	15.56	15.56	3.0	0.0	3.0	
31	Pakistan	6.22	6.89	7.78	20.89	20.89	13.93	2.50	2.00	3.00	2.00	9.50	9.50	2.5	3.0	4.0	2.0	11.5	11.5	3	13.93	9.50	11.50	-4.4	2.0	-2.4	f
32	Palau	–	–	1.33	–	3.50	2.33	2.00	2.00	2.00	2.00	8.00	8.00	2.0	2.0	2.0	3.0	9.0	9.0	2	2.33	8.00	9.00	5.7	1.0	6.7	d
33	Papua New Guinea	–	–	–	–	20.89	13.93	3.56	1.00	3.00	1.00	8.56	8.56	3.6	1.0	4.0	1.0	9.6	9.6	2	13.93	8.56	9.56	-5.4	1.0	-4.4	f
34	Philippines	6.56	6.89	6.44	19.89	19.89	13.26	2.94	2.50	3.00	2.50	10.94	10.94	2.9	3.0	3.0	2.5	11.4	11.4	2	13.26	10.94	11.44	-2.3	0.5	-1.8	
35	Samoa	–	–	–	–	9.00	6.00	1.50	3.00	ND	1.00	5.50	7.33	1.5	3.5	ND	1.0	6.0	8.0	2	6.00	7.33	8.00	1.3	0.7	2.0	
36	Singapore	–	8.89	5.78	–	14.67	9.78	3.25	5.00	5.00	5.00	18.25	18.25	3.3	5.0	5.0	5.0	18.3	18.3	4	9.78	18.25	18.25	8.5	0.0	8.5	e
37	Solomon Islands	–	–	9.56	–	14.67	9.78	2.25	3.00	ND	1.00	6.25	8.33	2.3	3.0	ND	1.0	6.3	8.3	2	9.78	8.33	8.33	-1.4	0.0	-1.4	
38	Sri Lanka	6.56	5.56	6.44	18.56	18.56	12.37	2.88	2.50	3.00	1.50	9.88	9.88	2.9	3.5	4.0	2.0	12.4	12.4	3	12.37	9.88	12.38	-2.5	2.5	0.0	
39	Taipei,China	–	–	–	–	15.00	10.00	3.33	4.00	3.00	3.00	13.33	13.33	3.0	5.0	3.0	ND	11.0	14.7	3	10.00	13.33	14.67	3.3	1.3	4.7	
40	Tajikistan	6.44	5.78	9.56	21.78	21.78	14.52	3.25	1.50	2.00	2.00	8.75	8.75	3.3	2.0	2.0	2.0	9.3	9.3	2	14.52	8.75	9.25	-5.8	0.5	-5.3	f
41	Thailand	5.89	6.22	5.11	17.22	17.22	11.48	3.69	3.00	4.00	3.00	13.69	13.69	3.7	3.5	5.0	3.5	15.7	15.7	4	11.48	13.69	15.69	2.2	2.0	4.2	
42	Timor-Leste	–	–	4.00	–	15.00	10.00	2.50	1.00	4.00	1.00	8.50	8.50	2.5	1.0	4.0	2.0	9.5	9.5	2	10.00	8.50	9.50	-1.5	1.0	-0.5	
43	Tonga	–	1.33	1.33	–	3.50	2.33	1.75	1.00	ND	1.00	3.75	5.00	1.8	1.0	ND	1.0	3.8	5.0	1	2.33	5.00	5.00	2.7	0.0	2.7	
44	Turkmenistan	5.00	5.33	6.67	17.00	17.00	11.33	2.38	2.50	3.00	3.50	11.38	11.38	2.4	3.0	4.0	5.0	14.4	14.4	3	11.33	11.38	14.38	0.0	3.0	3.0	
45	Tuvalu	–	–	1.33	–	3.50	2.33	2.00	4.00	ND	ND	6.00	12.00	2.0	4.0	1.0	1.0	8.0	8.0	2	2.33	12.00	8.00	9.7	-4.0	5.7	d
46	Uzbekistan	5.33	4.67	6.00	16.00	16.00	10.67	2.38	2.50	2.00	2.50	9.38	9.38	2.4	2.5	3.0	2.5	10.4	10.4	2	10.67	9.38	10.38	-1.3	1.0	-0.3	
47	Vanuatu	–	–	–	–	3.50	2.33	2.00	3.00	ND	1.00	6.00	8.00	2.3	3.0	2.0	1.0	8.3	8.3	2	2.33	8.00	8.33	5.7	0.3	6.0	
48	Viet Nam	5.11	4.44	6.22	15.78	15.78	10.52	3.56	2.50	3.00	2.00	11.06	11.06	3.6	3.5	4.0	1.5	12.6	12.6	3	10.52	11.06	12.56	0.5	1.5	2.0	
	sum												539						568		460	539	568	79.4	28.5	107.9	

Difference summary:

	2013adj–2013pub	2016–2013adj	2016–2013pub
sum	79.4	28.5	107.9
pos	110.8	38.5	125.3
neg	-31.4	-10.0	-17.5
sum	17.3%	5.3%	19.0%
pos	24.1%	7.1%	22.1%
neg	-6.8%	-1.9%	-3.1%

Rating by expert judgment (no data available)

Missing data – Overall score is adjusted by multiplying with 4/3 (one missing score) or 4/2 (2 missing scores)

Based on AWDO2013 index: 1=3.50; 2=-9; 3=15; 4=21

multiplied by 4/3

EO estimates Pacific Islands used

Source: ADB.

Table A3.3: Detailed Results for Urban Water Security (KD3)

#	Economy	AWDO 2013 (published)							AWDO 2013 (adjusted)						AWDO 2016						KD3 scores			Differences			Remarks
		Water Supply Index	Wastewater Treatment Index	Drainage Index	Urban Factor	River Health Index Factor	Indicator (20 pts max.)	Adj. KD3 score (16 pts)	Water Supply Index	Wastewater Treatment Index	Drainage Index	Urban Factor	River Health Index Factor	KD3 Score	Water Supply Index	Wastewater Treatment Index	Drainage Index	Urban Factor	River Health Index Factor	KD3 score	2013pub	2013 adj	2016	2013adj–2013pub	2016–2013adj	2016–2013pub	
1	Afghanistan	1	1	4	0.8	0	4.8	4.8	1	1	4	0.8	0	4.8	1	1	4	0.8	0	4.8	4.8	4.8	4.8	0.0	0.0	0.0	
2	Armenia	5	1	5	1.0	0	11.0	11.0	5	5	5	1.0	0	14.0	5	4	4	1.0	0	13.0	11.0	14.0	13.0	3.0	-1.0	2.0	
3	Australia	5	5	4	1.0	1	19.0	15.0	5	5	4	1.0	1	15.0	4	5	4	1.0	1	15.0	15.0	15.0	15.0	0.0	0.0	0.0	
4	Azerbaijan	3	1	4	1.0	0	8.0	8.0	4	1	5	1.0	0	10.0	4	1	5	1.0	0	10.0	8.0	10.0	10.0	2.0	0.0	2.0	
5	Bangladesh	1	1	1	0.8	0	2.4	2.4	1	1	1	0.8	0	2.4	1	1	3	0.8	0	4.0	2.4	2.4	4.0	0.0	1.6	1.6	a
6	Bhutan	4	1	5	0.8	1	12.0	8.8	4	1	5	0.8	0	8.0	5	1	5	0.8	0	7.2	8.8	8.0	7.2	-0.8	-0.8	-1.6	
7	Brunei Darussalam	5	5	5	0.9	1	18.0	14.4	5	5	5	0.9	0	13.5	5	5	5	1.0	0	15.0	14.4	13.5	15.0	-0.9	1.5	0.6	b
8	Cambodia	2	1	2	0.8	0	4.0	4.0	3	1	3	0.8	0	4.8	3	1	3	0.8	0	4.5	4.0	4.8	4.5	0.8	-0.3	0.5	
9	China, People's Republic of	5	1	4	0.9	1	9.0	9.0	4	4	4	1.0	0	9.0	4	4	4	0.9	0	10.8	9.0	9.0	10.8	0.0	1.8	1.8	c + d
10	Cook Islands	5	1	5	1.0	0	12.0	8.0	3	3	5	0.9	0	9.9	5	3	5	0.9	0	12.0	8.0	9.9	12.0	1.9	2.1	4.0	b + d
11	Fiji	5	1	1	1.0	0	7.0	7.0	5	3	3	1.0	1	12.0	5	3	2	1.0	1	11.0	7.0	12.0	11.0	5.0	-1.0	4.0	e
12	Georgia	5	3	5	1.0	1	13.0	13.0	5	3	5	1.0	0	13.0	4	4	4	1.0	0	12.0	13.0	13.0	12.0	0.0	-1.0	-1.0	e
13	Hong Kong, China	5	5	5	1.0	1	20.0	16.0	5	5	5	1.0	0	15.0	5	5	5	1.0	0	15.0	16.0	15.0	15.0	-1.0	0.0	-1.0	
14	India	1	1	4	0.9	0	4.5	4.5	1	1	4	0.9	0	5.4	1	3	4	0.9	0	4.5	4.5	5.4	4.5	0.9	-0.9	0.0	e
15	Indonesia	1	1	4	0.8	1	8.8	5.6	1	1	4	0.8	1	5.6	5	1	4	0.9	1	6.3	5.6	5.6	6.3	0.0	0.7	0.7	b
16	Japan	5	5	4	1.0	0	14.0	14.0	5	5	4	1.0	0	14.0	5	3	4	1.0	0	12.0	14.0	14.0	12.0	0.0	-2.0	-2.0	
17	Kazakhstan	4	1	4	1.0	0	9.0	9.0	5	1	5	1.0	0	11.0	5	1	5	1.0	0	12.0	9.0	11.0	12.0	2.0	1.0	3.0	c
18	Kiribati	5	1	5	0.8	0	5.6	5.6	5	1	5	0.8	0	6.4	2	1	5	1.0	0	8.0	5.6	6.4	8.0	0.8	1.6	2.4	f
19	Korea, Republic of	5	2	4	1.0	1	11.0	11.0	5	2	4	1.0	0	9.6	5	3	4	1.0	0	12.0	11.0	9.6	12.0	-1.4	2.4	1.0	b
20	Kyrgyz Republic	4	1	5	1.0	0	10.0	10.0	4	1	5	1.0	0	11.0	4	2	5	1.0	0	11.0	10.0	11.0	11.0	1.0	0.0	1.0	
21	Lao People's Democratic Republic	1	1	1	0.8	1	6.4	3.2	4	2	5	0.8	0	6.0	4	2	4	0.8	0	6.4	3.2	6.0	6.4	2.8	0.4	3.2	
22	Malaysia	5	3	4	0.8	1	13.6	10.4	5	5	5	0.8	0	11.2	5	5	5	0.9	0	12.6	10.4	11.2	12.6	0.8	1.4	2.2	b
23	Maldives	5	1	4	0.8	0	12.0	8.8	5	2	5	0.8	0	9.6	5	2	5	0.8	0	9.6	8.8	9.6	9.6	0.8	0.0	0.8	b
24	Marshall Islands	5	1	1	0.9	1	10.8	7.2	5	2	5	0.8	0	6.4	5	2	5	0.8	0	8.0	7.2	6.4	8.0	-0.8	1.6	0.8	b
25	Micronesia, Federated States of	5	2	3	1.0	1	15.0	11.0	4	2	4	1.0	0	7.0	4	2	4	1.0	0	7.0	11.0	7.0	7.0	-4.0	0.0	-4.0	b + d
26	Mongolia	1	1	3	1.0	0	10.0	6.0	1	1	4	0.9	1	6.3	1	1	4	0.9	1	6.3	6.0	6.3	6.3	0.3	0.0	0.3	
27	Myanmar	1	1	1	0.9	1	7.2	3.6	1	1	1	1.0	1	4.0	1	1	1	0.9	1	2.7	3.6	4.0	2.7	0.4	-1.3	-0.9	b
28	Nauru	1	1	4	1.0	0	6.0	6.0	5	1	5	1.0	0	8.0	5	1	5	1.0	0	8.0	6.0	8.0	8.0	2.0	0.0	2.0	b + e
29	Nepal	1	1	4	0.8	0	4.8	4.8	1	1	4	0.9	0	5.4	1	1	4	0.9	0	4.8	4.8	5.4	4.8	0.6	-0.6	0.0	
30	New Zealand	5	5	5	1.0	1	19.0	15.0	5	5	5	1.0	0	16.0	5	5	5	1.0	0	15.0	15.0	16.0	15.0	1.0	-1.0	0.0	b + e
31	Pakistan	1	1	4	0.8	0	4.8	4.8	2	1	5	0.9	0	6.0	2	1	4	0.9	0	3.6	4.8	6.0	3.6	1.2	-2.4	-1.2	b + e
32	Palau	1	2	1	1.0	0	9.0	5.0	5	3	5	1.0	0	14.0	5	3	5	1.0	0	14.0	5.0	14.0	14.0	9.0	0.0	9.0	c
33	Papua New Guinea	2	1	4	0.9	0	9.9	6.3	1	1	5	0.9	0	6.4	1	1	4	0.9	1	6.3	6.3	6.4	6.3	0.1	-0.1	0.0	b + e
34	Philippines	2	1	5	0.8	0	5.6	5.6	2	2	5	0.9	0	6.3	1	2	2	0.9	0	4.0	5.6	6.3	4.0	0.7	-2.3	-1.6	b
35	Samoa	4	1	4	1.0	0	9.0	9.0	4	1	4	1.0	0	12.0	5	3	4	1.0	0	9.0	9.0	12.0	9.0	3.0	-3.0	0.0	e
36	Singapore	5	5	5	1.0	1	15.0	15.0	5	5	5	1.0	0	15.0	5	5	5	1.0	0	15.0	15.0	15.0	15.0	0.0	0.0	0.0	
37	Solomon Islands	3	1	4	1.0	0	10.0	6.0	3	2	4	0.8	1	10.0	1	2	4	0.8	1	6.4	6.0	10.0	6.4	4.0	-3.6	0.4	e
38	Sri Lanka	2	1	4	1.0	0	7.0	7.0	4	2	4	1.0	0	8.0	3	2	4	1.0	0	8.0	7.0	8.0	8.0	1.0	0.0	1.0	
39	Taipei,China	5	1	5	1.0	1	16.0	12.0	5	1	5	1.0	0	11.0	5	1	4	1.0	0	10.0	12.0	11.0	10.0	-1.0	-1.0	-2.0	e
40	Tajikistan	4	1	3	1.0	0	11.0	7.0	3	2	4	1.0	1	9.0	4	1	3	1.0	1	7.2	7.0	9.0	7.2	2.0	-1.8	0.2	b + e
41	Thailand	4	2	4	1.0	0	10.0	10.0	3	2	4	1.0	0	9.0	3	2	2	1.0	0	5.4	10.0	9.0	5.4	-1.0	-3.6	-4.6	b + e
42	Timor-Leste	1	1	1	0.8	1	8.8	5.6	1	1	5	0.8	1	6.4	1	1	5	0.8	1	5.6	5.6	6.4	5.6	0.8	-0.8	0.0	d
43	Tonga	5	3	1	1.0	0	9.0	9.0	3	3	1	1.0	0	7.0	3	3	1	1.0	0	7.0	9.0	7.0	7.0	-2.0	0.0	-2.0	c
44	Turkmenistan	4	1	4	0.8	0	8.0	8.0	4	3	5	0.9	1	8.8	4	3	5	0.9	1	11.7	8.0	8.8	11.7	0.8	2.9	3.7	
45	Tuvalu	5	1	2	0.9	0	7.2	7.2	5	2	5	1.0	0	10.8	5	2	5	1.0	0	12.0	7.2	10.8	12.0	3.6	1.2	4.8	b
46	Uzbekistan	4	1	5	1.0	0	10.0	10.0	4	1	5	1.0	0	10.0	4	1	5	1.0	0	10.0	10.0	10.0	10.0	0.0	0.0	0.0	
47	Vanuatu	1	1	3	1.0	0	10.0	6.0	2	1	5	0.8	1	8.0	2	1	5	0.8	1	7.2	6.0	8.0	7.2	2.0	-0.8	1.2	b
48	Viet Nam	1	1	1	0.8	0	2.4	2.4	1	1	4	0.8	0	4.8	2	1	2	0.8	0	4.0	2.4	4.8	4.0	2.4	-0.8	1.6	e
																					393	437	427				

sum 43.8 | -9.9 | 33.9
pos. 56.7 | 20.2 | 55.8
neg. -12.9 | -30.1 | -21.9
sum 11.1% | -2.3% | 7.9%
pos. 14.4% | 4.6% | 13.1%
neg. -3.3% | -6.9% | -5.1%

Expert estimates made for AWDO 2013
Estimates made by IWC

Source: ADB.

Table A3.4: Detailed Results for Environmental Water Security (KD4)

#	Economy	AWDO 2013 (2000) (published)			AWDO 2013 (2000) (adjusted)			AWDO 2016 (2010)						KD4 scores			Differences		
		RHI	KD4 Index	Est. 15 Pts.	RHI	KD4 Index	Est. 15 Pts.	RHI	RHI score	Flow	Gover-nance	Score max. 15pts	exp.	2013pub	2103 adj	2016	2013adj-2013pub	2016-2013adj	2016-2013pub
1	Afghanistan	0.33	2	5.0	0.32	2	4.8	0.32	2	1	1	4		5.0	4.8	4	−0.2	−0.8	−1.0
2	Armenia	0.08	1	3.0	0.13	1	3.0	0.14	1	1	5	7		3.0	3.0	7	0.0	4.0	4.0
3	Australia	0.59	4	8.9	0.61	4	9.2	0.61	4	3	5	12		8.9	9.2	12	0.3	2.9	3.2
4	Azerbaijan	0.13	1	3.0	0.13	1	3.0	0.15	1	1	3	5		3.0	3.0	5	0.0	2.0	2.0
5	Bangladesh	0.16	1	3.0	0.06	1	3.0	0.01	1	1	2	4		3.0	3.0	4	0.0	1.0	1.0
6	Bhutan	0.39	3	5.9	0.29	2	4.4	0.27	2	4	2	8		5.9	4.4	8	−1.5	3.7	2.2
7	Brunei Darussalam	0.52	3	7.8	0.30	2	4.5	0.25	2	5	4	11		7.8	4.5	11	−3.3	6.5	3.2
8	Cambodia	0.29	2	4.4	0.32	2	4.8	0.30	2	2	2	6		4.4	4.8	6	0.5	1.2	1.7
9	China, People's Republic of	0.26	2	3.9	0.29	2	4.4	0.26	2	2	2	6		3.9	4.4	6	0.4	1.7	2.1
10	Cook Islands	–	3	9.0	–	–	9.0	0.57	4	–	–	12	12	9.0	9.0	12	0.0	3.0	3.0
11	Fiji	–	2	6.0	0.57	4	8.6	0.54	4	5	2	11	9	6.0	8.6	11	2.6	2.5	5.0
12	Georgia	0.26	2	3.9	0.23	2	3.5	0.24	2	3	2	7		3.9	3.5	7	−0.5	3.6	3.1
13	Hong Kong, China	–	3	9.0	–	–	9.0	0.00	1	–	–	9	???	9.0	9.0	9	0.0	0.0	0.0
14	India	0.11	1	3.0	0.11	1	3.0	0.07	1	1	2	4		3.0	3.0	4	0.0	1.0	1.0
15	Indonesia	0.46	3	6.9	0.48	3	7.2	0.42	3	4	3	10		6.9	7.2	10	0.3	2.8	3.1
16	Japan	0.23	2	3.5	0.28	2	4.2	0.27	2	2	5	9		3.5	4.2	9	0.8	4.8	5.6
17	Kazakhstan	0.35	2	5.3	0.42	3	6.3	0.40	3	4	2	9		5.3	6.3	9	1.1	2.7	3.8
18	Kiribati	–	1	4.0	–	–	4.0	–	–	–	2	3	3	4.0	4.0	3	0.0	−1.0	−1.0
19	Korea, Republic of	–	2	6.0	0.11	1	3.0	0.06	1	1	4	6		6.0	3.0	6	−3.0	3.0	0.0
20	Kyrgyz Republic	–	2	6.0	0.33	2	5.0	0.32	2	1	2	5		6.0	5.0	5	−1.1		−1.0
21	Lao People's Democratic Republic	0.38	3	5.7	0.34	2	5.1	0.31	2	2	2	6		5.7	5.1	6	−0.6	0.9	0.3
22	Malaysia	0.41	3	6.2	0.32	2	4.8	0.27	2	5	3	10		6.2	4.8	10	−1.4	5.2	3.9
23	Maldives	–	4	12.0	–	–	12.0	–	–	–	–	12	???	12.0	12.0	12	0.0	0.0	0.0
24	Marshall Islands	–	4	12.0	–	–	12.0	–	–	–	–	9	9	12.0	12.0	9	0.0	−3.0	−3.0
25	Micronesia, Federated States of	–	3	9.0	–	–	9.0	–	–	–	–	12	12	9.0	9.0	12	0.0	3.0	3.0
26	Mongolia	0.57	4	8.6	0.61	4	9.2	0.58	4	3	2	9		8.6	9.2	9	0.6	−0.2	0.4
27	Myanmar	0.39	3	5.9	0.39	3	5.9	0.36	3	3	2	8		5.9	5.9	8	0.0	2.2	2.2
28	Nauru	–	2	6.0	–	–	6.0	–	v	–	–	12	15	6.0	6.0	12	0.0	6.0	6.0
29	Nepal	0.26	2	3.9	0.22	2	3.3	0.20	1	3	4	8		3.9	3.3	8	−0.6	4.7	4.1
30	New Zealand	0.54	4	8.1	0.38	3	5.7	0.36	3	5	5	13		8.1	5.7	13	−2.4	7.3	4.9
31	Pakistan	0.12	1	3.0	0.17	1	3.0	0.14	1	1	3	5		3.0	3.0	5	0.0	2.0	2.0
32	Palau	–	3	9.0	0.54	3	8.1	0.53	3	–	3	11	12	9.0	8.1	11	−0.9	2.9	2.0
33	Papua New Guinea	0.64	4	9.6	0.69	4	10.4	0.62	4	5	1	10	12	9.6	10.4	10	0.8	−0.4	0.4
34	Philippines	0.35	2	5.3	0.19	1	3.0	0.15	1	2	3	6		5.3	3.0	6	−2.3	3.0	0.8
35	Samoa	–	2	6.0	0.23	2	3.5	0.23	2	–	–	10	12	6.0	3.5	10	−2.6	6.6	4.0
36	Singapore	0.27	2	4.1	0.28	2	4.2	0.20	1	5	5	11		4.1	4.2	11	0.1	6.8	7.0
37	Solomon Islands	0.92	5	13.8	0.93	5	14.0	0.93	5	5	1	11	12	13.8	14.0	11	0.2	−3.0	−2.8
38	Sri Lanka	0.20	1	3.0	0.15	1	3.0	0.13	1	1	4	6		3.0	3.0	6	0.0	3.0	3.0
39	Taipei,China	–	3	9.0	0.21	1	3.2	0.16	1	2	4	7		9.0	3.2	7	−5.9	3.9	−2.0
40	Tajikistan	0.35	2	5.3	0.41	3	6.2	0.39	3	4	2	9		5.3	6.2	9	0.9	2.9	3.8
41	Thailand	0.16	1	3.0	0.17	1	3.0	0.15	1	1	4	6		3.0	3.0	6	0.0	3.0	3.0
42	Timor-Leste	0.37	3	5.6	0.41	3	6.2	0.17	1	2	2	5	9	5.6	6.2	5	0.6	−1.2	−0.6
43	Tonga	–	2	6.0	0.32	2	4.8	0.32	2	–	2	6	6	6.0	4.8	6	−1.2	1.2	0.0
44	Turkmenistan	0.36	2	5.4	0.40	3	6.0	0.37	3	2	1	6		5.4	6.0	6	0.6	0.0	0.6
45	Tuvalu	–	2	6.0	–	–	6.0	–	–	–	–	12	12	6.0	6.0	12	0.0	6.0	6.0
46	Uzbekistan	0.28	2	4.2	0.35	2	5.3	0.33	2	3	1	6		4.2	5.3	6	1.1	0.8	1.8
47	Vanuatu	0.90	5	13.5	0.67	4	10.1	0.67	4	5	2	11	9	13.5	10.1	11	−3.5	0.9	−2.5
48	Viet Nam	0.27	2	4.1	0.12	1	3.0	0.09	1	1	2	4		4.1	3.0	4	−1.1	1.0	−0.1
	KD-Index Rating by expert judgment no. (no data available)			300.1			279.1					389.0		300.0	279.0	389	sum −21.0	109.9	88.9
																	pos. 10.7	119.3	102.8
																	neg. −31.7	−9.4	−13.9
																	sum −7.0%	39.4%	22.9%
																	pos. 3.5%	42.7%	26.4%
																	neg. −10.5%	−3.4%	−3.6%

Scores given for:
2013 1 4
       2 6
       3 9
       4 12

Also applied: minimum score of 3

ass: same values as 2013

assumption same value as 2013adj

Source: ADB.

The following conclusions were drawn from the results for KD4:

- The impact of the changed methodology shows the impact of the change in the RHI only. The impact is that the scores are somewhat lower (average 7%).
- The differences between AWDO 2016 and AWDO 2013 are major and ranges from +40% to −40%. This change is most likely caused by the introduction of the two new flow alteration and governance subindicators.

5 Results and Comparison for Resilience to Water-Related Disasters (KD5)

Table A3.5 presents the detailed results for KD5 in terms of scores on a 0–3 scale. The coloring of the scores indicates how missing data have been dealt with. This is explained in the main text of this methodology report.

The differences in scores between the three cases are given in the three rightmost columns. The coloring in these columns indicates the direction and size of the difference: green for higher scores and red for lower scores.

The adjustment in the methodology to determine KD5 has been minor (see the main text on KD5 for a description of this adjustment).

The following conclusions were drawn from the results for KD5:

- The impact of the (slightly) changed methodology is limited; the average score decreased by 2%.
- The difference between AWDO 2016 and AWDO 2013 is major and in the order of 40%. Major changes can be found for small island countries.

6 Comparison of Key Dimensions and National Water Security Index Results Based on Scores

The scores of the five key dimensions have been made comparable by adjusting the scores from their original range to the standard 1–20 range. The following tables present the results for the three cases:

- Table A3.6 – Summary of key dimension scores (maximum of 20)
- Table A3.7 – Differences in scores for the three cases
- Table A3.8 – Count table differences in scores for the three cases

Table A3.6 provides an overview of the key dimension scores presented in the previous section, now adjusted to a maximum 20 scale for all. The NWSI is the sum of the key dimension scores and has a maximum score of 100.

The more interesting table is Table A3.7 which presents the differences in the key dimension and NWS scores. These differences are given without digits. The accuracy of the numbers does not justify drawing conclusions on differences smaller than 5%. The coloring indicates the changes (green for up and red for down) and the intensity of the color the size of the change.

Basically, these tables provide the same information as given in sections 1–5, but now as overview of all key dimensions together with the NWSI.

- The tables show that the impact of the changed methodology is mainly in KD2, KD3, and KD4, with KD2 and KD3 providing somewhat higher scores and KD4 somewhat lower scores. In particular, the small island countries show major changes in their scores.
- The applied changes in methodology also mean that the NWSI has gone up somewhat (average 2 points on a 100-point scale).

Table A3.5: Detailed Results Resilience to Water-Related Disasters (KD5)

#	Economy	AWDO 2013 (published) Flood and Wind Storm Resilience Indicator (0–1)	Drought Resilience Indicator (0–1)	Storm surge/coastal flood Resilience Indicator (0–1)	Water Related Disaster Resilience Indicator	Est. 15 Pts.	KD5	AWDO 2013 (adjusted) Flood and Wind Storm Resilience Indicator (0–1)	Drought Resilience Indicator (0–1)	Storm surge/coastal flood Resilience Indicator (0–1)	Water Related Disaster Resilience Indicator (0–3)	Est. 15 Pts.	AWDO 2016 Flood and Wind Storm Resilience Indicator (0–1)	Drought Resilience Indicator (0–1)	Storm surge/coastal flood Resilience Indicator (0–1)	Water Related Disaster Resilience Indicator (0–3)	Est. 15 Pts.	KD2 2013pub	KD2 2103adj	KD2 2016	Diff 2013adj–2013pub	Diff 2016–2013adj	Diff 2016–2013pub
1	Afghanistan	0.55	0.42			2.00	1					2.00	0.20	0.20	0.20	0.60	3.0	2.00	2.00	3.00	0.0	1.0	1.0
2	Armenia	1.00		1.00	0.97	4.84	2	0.45	0.33	1.00	1.79	8.93	0.57	0.51	0.54	1.62	8.1	4.84	8.93	8.09	4.1	-0.8	3.3
3	Australia	0.42	0.33	0.24	3.00	14.99	5	1.00	1.00	1.00	3.00	15.00	0.92	1.00	1.00	2.92	14.6	14.99	15.00	14.58	0.0	-0.4	-0.4
4	Azerbaijan	0.22	0.16	0.13	0.98	4.92	2	0.29	0.23	0.35	0.88	4.38	0.39	0.36	0.37	1.12	5.6	4.92	4.38	5.60	-0.5	1.2	0.7
5	Bangladesh				0.51	2.56	2	0.05	0.04	0.20	0.29	1.44	0.20	0.20	0.24	0.64	3.2	2.56	1.44	3.18	-1.1	1.7	0.6
6	Bhutan					4.00	3					4.00	0.40	0.40	0.40	1.20	6.0	4.00	4.00	6.00	0.0	2.0	2.0
7	Brunei Darussalam				1.22	6.09	3	0.34	0.31	0.54	1.19	5.95	0.55	0.51	0.65	1.71	8.6	6.09	5.95	8.57	-0.1	2.6	2.5
8	Cambodia				0.47	2.34	1	0.02	0.02	0.19	0.23	1.16	0.20	0.20	0.28	0.68	3.4	2.34	1.16	3.39	-1.2	2.2	1.1
9	China, People's Republic of				1.07	5.34	3	0.06	0.04	0.48	0.58	2.88	0.49	0.39	0.68	1.56	7.8	5.34	2.88	7.81	-2.5	4.9	2.5
10	Cook Islands					2.00	1					2.00	0.60	0.80	0.40	1.80	9.0	2.00	2.00	9.00	0.0	7.0	7.0
11	Fiji	0.44	0.34	0.29	1.07	5.37	3	0.02	0.02	0.43	0.47	2.37	0.57	0.47	0.67	1.71	8.5	5.37	2.37	8.55	-3.0	6.2	3.2
12	Georgia	0.74	0.59	0.46	1.79	8.95	3	0.69	0.52	0.67	1.88	9.41	0.76	0.64	0.71	2.11	10.5	8.95	9.41	10.53	0.5	1.1	1.6
13	Hong Kong, China	0.51	0.42	0.47	1.40	7.02	3	0.69	0.52	0.67	1.88	9.41	0.63	0.45	0.71	1.78	8.9	7.02	9.41	8.90	2.4	-0.5	1.9
14	India	0.28	0.21	0.20	0.69	3.44	2	0.13	0.09	0.29	0.51	2.56	0.20	0.20	0.39	0.79	3.9	3.44	2.56	3.94	-0.9	1.4	0.5
15	Indonesia	0.31	0.27	0.27	0.85	4.24	2	0.16	0.16	0.40	0.72	3.61	0.26	0.23	0.46	0.95	4.7	4.24	3.61	4.74	-0.6	1.1	0.5
16	Japan	0.90	0.81	0.72	2.44	12.18	4	0.87	0.79	1.00	2.66	13.30	0.98	0.94	1.00	2.92	14.6	12.18	13.30	14.62	1.1	1.3	2.4
17	Kazakhstan	0.77	0.69	0.54	2.00	10.01	4	0.72	0.65	0.79	2.16	10.80	0.69	0.69	0.69	2.07	10.4	10.01	10.80	10.35	0.8	-0.4	0.3
18	Kiribati	0.18	0.14	0.56	0.88	4.42	1	0.01	0.02	0.15	0.18	0.89	0.20	0.40	0.20	0.80	4.0	4.42	0.89	4.00	-3.5	3.1	-0.4
19	Korea, Republic of	0.67	0.57	0.23	1.47	7.36	3	0.16	0.14	0.83	1.12	5.62	0.78	0.71	0.88	2.37	11.9	7.36	5.62	11.87	-1.7	6.2	4.5
20	Kyrgyz Republic	0.38	0.27		0.64	3.22	2	0.01	0.02	1.00	1.03	5.13	0.34	0.25	0.29	0.87	4.4	3.22	5.13	4.36	1.9	-0.8	1.1
21	Lao People's Democratic Republic					7.00	3	0.02	0.01	1.00	1.03	5.17	0.20	0.20	0.20	0.60	3.0	7.00	5.17	3.00	-1.8	-2.2	-4.0
22	Malaysia	0.38	0.31	0.31	1.00	4.98	2	0.24	0.21	0.46	0.91	4.98	0.39	0.35	0.58	1.33	6.6	4.98	4.98	6.63	0.0	1.7	1.7
23	Maldives					2.00	1					2.00	0.20	0.20	0.20	0.60	3.0	2.00	2.00	3.00	0.0	1.0	1.0
24	Marshall Islands					2.00	1					2.00	0.40	0.40	0.20	1.00	5.0	2.00	2.00	5.00	0.0	3.0	3.0
25	Micronesia, Federated States of					4.00	2					4.00	0.40	0.60	0.60	1.60	8.0	4.00	4.00	8.00	0.0	4.0	4.0
26	Mongolia	0.36	0.27		0.63	3.14	2	0.22	0.16		1.38	3.14	0.38	0.33	0.35	1.06	5.3	3.14	3.14	5.30	0.0	2.2	2.2
27	Myanmar					2.00	1			1.00		2.00	0.40	0.20	0.20	0.80	4.0	2.00	2.00	4.00	0.0	2.0	2.0
28	Nauru					4.00	2					4.00	0.80	0.80	1.00	2.60	13.0	4.00	4.00	13.00	0.0	9.0	9.0
29	Nepal	0.17	0.13		0.30	1.52	1	0.00	0.00	1.00	1.00	1.52	0.20	0.20	0.20	0.60	3.0	1.52	1.52	3.00	0.0	1.5	1.5
30	New Zealand	1.00	0.87	0.82	2.69	13.44	5	1.00	0.85	1.00	2.85	14.23	1.00	0.95	1.00	2.95	14.8	13.44	14.23	14.77	0.8	0.5	1.3
31	Pakistan	0.23	0.17	0.17	0.58	2.88	2	0.07	0.05	0.25	0.37	2.88	0.20	0.20	0.30	0.70	3.5	2.88	2.88	3.50	0.0	0.6	0.6
32	Palau					4.00	2					4.00	0.80	0.40	0.60	1.80	9.0	4.00	4.00	9.00	0.0	5.0	5.0
33	Papua New Guinea	0.23	0.16	0.14	0.53	2.65	2	0.06	0.04	0.21	0.31	1.55	0.20	0.20	0.30	0.70	3.5	2.65	1.55	3.51	-1.1	2.0	0.9
34	Philippines	0.30	0.25	0.23	0.78	3.91	2	0.16	0.14	0.34	0.63	3.17	0.32	0.25	0.42	1.00	5.0	3.91	3.17	4.98	-0.7	1.8	1.1
35	Samoa	0.41	0.28	0.26	0.95	4.77	3	0.28	0.17	0.39	0.85	4.24	0.22	0.20	0.40	0.82	4.1	4.77	4.24	4.08	-0.5	-0.2	-0.7
36	Singapore	0.59	0.47	0.45	1.51	7.56	3	0.51	0.39	0.67	1.57	7.85	0.57	0.48	0.64	1.69	8.4	7.56	7.85	8.45	0.3	0.6	0.9
37	Solomon Islands					2.00	1					2.00	0.40	0.80	0.80	2.00	10.0	2.00	2.00	10.00	0.0	8.0	8.0
38	Sri Lanka	0.43	0.34	0.29	1.06	5.30	3	0.31	0.24	0.43	0.98	5.30	0.36	0.32	0.47	1.15	5.8	5.30	5.30	5.76	0.0	0.5	0.5
39	Taipei,China	0.77	0.62	0.51	1.90	9.50	3	0.72	0.57	0.76	2.04	10.20	0.95	0.66	0.86	2.46	12.3	9.50	10.20	12.32	0.7	2.1	2.8
40	Tajikistan	0.32	0.23		0.55	2.74	3	0.17	0.12	1.00	1.29	6.45	0.23	0.20	0.21	0.64	3.2	2.74	6.45	3.19	3.7	-3.3	0.4
41	Thailand	0.51	0.42	0.35	1.28	6.38	3	0.41	0.33	0.51	1.25	6.26	0.51	0.42	0.66	1.59	7.9	6.38	6.26	7.94	-0.1	1.7	1.6
42	Timor-Leste					2.00	1					2.00	0.60	0.80	0.80	2.20	11.0	2.00	2.00	11.00	0.0	9.0	9.0
43	Tonga	0.35	0.25	0.23	0.84	4.18	2	0.22	0.14	0.34	0.70	4.18	0.21	0.30	0.37	0.78	3.9	4.18	4.18	3.89	0.0	-0.3	-0.3
44	Turkmenistan	0.37	0.28	0.24	0.89	4.46	2	0.23	0.18	0.36	0.77	3.83	0.21	0.40	0.20	0.76	3.8	4.46	3.83	3.81	-0.6	-0.2	-0.6
45	Tuvalu					2.00	1					2.00	0.20	0.20	0.20	0.80	4.0	2.00	2.00	4.00	0.0	2.0	2.0
46	Uzbekistan	0.37	0.27	0.25	0.90	4.50	2	0.24	0.16	0.38	0.78	4.50	0.34	0.26	0.30	0.89	4.5	4.50	4.50	4.45	0.0	0.0	0.0
47	Vanuatu	0.18	0.14	0.14	0.46	2.32	1	0.01	0.01	0.21	0.23	1.15	0.20	0.20	0.30	0.70	3.5	2.32	1.15	3.51	-1.2	2.4	1.2
48	Viet Nam	0.36	0.31	0.20	0.87	4.35	2	0.22	0.21	0.29	0.73	3.64	0.28	0.32	0.39	0.99	5.0	4.35	3.64	4.96	-0.7	1.3	0.6
	sum																	235.00	229.00	325.00	-5.7	96.0	90.3
	pos.																				16.3	105.0	96.8
	neg.																				-22.0	-8.9	-6.5
																					-2.4%	41.9%	27.8%
																					6.9%	45.8%	29.8%
																					-9.4%	-3.9%	-2.0%

Assumption: same value as 2013

Assumption score:

1	1
2	2
3	3

1	2
2	4
3	7

Legend:
- estimates by AWDO team
- estimates by other experts
- expert
- corrections for land-locked countries
- minimum value of 1 given (on 5pts scale)

Source: ADB.

- Progress in scores between (adjusted) AWDO 2013 and AWDO 2016 is seen for all key dimensions except KD3, which shows a slight decrease.

- The overall progress in national water security between AWDO 2013 and AWDO 2016 (which actually shows the progress of 5 years, see section 3.2) is about 6 points (on a 100-point scale).

Table A3.6: Summary of Key Dimension Scores (maximum 20 points)

Economy	AWDO 2013 (published)						AWDO 2013 (adjusted)						AWDO 2016					
	KD1 Rating	KD2 Rating	KD3 Rating	KD4 Rating	KD5 Rating	NWSI (average)	KD1 Rating	KD2 Rating	KD3 Rating	KD4 Rating	KD5 Rating	NWSI (average)	KD1 Rating	KD2 Rating	KD3 Rating	KD4 Rating	KD5 Rating	NWSI (average)
MAX	20	20	20	20	20	100	20	20	20	20	20	100	20	20	20	20	20	100
Afghanistan	4.0	6.0	6.0	6.6	2.7	25.3	4.0	8.1	6.0	6.4	2.7	27.2	4.0	8.1	6.0	5.3	4.0	27.5
Armenia	17.3	12.8	13.8	4.0	6.5	54.4	16.0	11.1	17.5	4.0	11.9	60.5	18.7	13.1	16.3	9.3	10.8	68.1
Australia	20.0	11.5	18.8	11.8	20.0	82.0	20.0	16.6	18.8	12.2	20.0	87.5	20.0	16.6	18.8	16.0	19.4	90.8
Azerbaijan	8.0	12.6	10.0	4.0	6.6	41.2	8.0	12.7	12.5	4.0	5.8	43.0	12.0	12.2	12.5	6.7	7.5	50.8
Bangladesh	4.0	9.5	3.0	4.0	3.4	23.9	4.0	12.1	3.0	4.0	1.9	25.0	4.0	14.1	5.0	5.3	4.2	35.3
Bhutan	4.0	11.1	11.0	7.8	5.3	39.2	4.0	14.2	10.0	5.8	5.3	39.3	6.7	14.2	9.0	10.7	8.0	48.5
Brunei Darussalam	18.7	6.0	18.0	10.4	8.1	61.2	20.0	14.3	16.9	6.0	7.9	65.1	20.0	14.3	18.8	14.7	11.4	79.1
Cambodia	4.0	9.5	5.0	5.8	3.1	27.4	4.0	13.7	6.0	6.4	1.5	31.6	6.7	12.7	5.6	8.0	4.5	37.5
China, People's Republic of	9.3	13.7	11.3	5.2	7.1	46.6	10.7	12.8	11.3	5.8	3.8	44.3	14.7	15.3	13.5	8.0	10.4	61.8
Cook Islands	18.7	6.0	10.0	12.0	2.7	49.3	16.0	5.5	12.4	12.0	2.7	48.5	16.0	6.8	15.0	16.0	12.0	65.8
Fiji	16.0	11.7	8.8	8.0	7.2	51.6	13.3	11.8	15.0	11.4	3.2	54.7	14.7	11.8	13.8	14.7	11.4	66.3
Georgia	13.3	10.4	16.3	5.2	11.9	57.2	12.0	10.0	16.3	4.6	12.6	55.4	16.0	10.5	15.0	9.3	14.0	64.9
Hong Kong, China	17.3	14.0	20.0	12.0	9.4	72.7	18.7	14.7	18.8	12.0	12.6	76.6	18.7	14.7	18.8	12.0	11.9	76.0
India	4.0	11.2	5.6	4.0	4.6	29.4	4.0	11.4	6.8	4.0	3.4	29.5	4.0	12.9	5.6	5.3	5.3	33.1
Indonesia	6.7	13.0	7.0	9.2	5.6	41.6	6.7	12.8	7.0	9.6	4.8	40.9	8.0	14.3	7.9	13.3	6.3	49.8
Japan	20.0	13.6	17.5	4.6	16.2	72.0	20.0	13.8	17.5	5.6	17.7	74.6	20.0	14.3	15.0	12.0	19.5	80.7
Kazakhstan	9.3	14.3	11.3	7.0	13.3	55.2	10.7	14.8	13.8	8.4	14.4	62.0	14.7	14.8	15.0	12.0	13.8	70.2
Kiribati	4.0	2.3	7.0	5.3	5.9	24.6	4.0	6.7	8.0	5.3	1.2	25.2	4.0	7.3	10.0	4.0	5.3	30.7
Korea, Republic of	18.7	11.6	13.8	8.0	9.8	61.8	18.7	15.6	12.0	4.0	7.5	57.8	20.0	15.6	15.0	8.0	15.8	74.4
Kyrgyz Republic	9.3	11.3	12.5	8.0	4.3	45.4	9.3	11.3	13.8	6.6	6.8	47.8	13.3	12.3	13.8	6.7	5.8	51.9
Lao People's Democratic Republic	5.3	12.2	4.0	7.6	9.3	38.5	4.0	9.8	7.5	6.8	6.9	35.0	6.7	11.3	8.0	8.0	4.0	38.0
Malaysia	18.7	14.2	13.0	8.2	6.6	60.7	18.7	14.9	14.0	6.4	6.6	60.6	20.0	15.4	15.8	13.3	8.8	73.4
Maldives	10.7	2.3	11.0	16.0	2.7	42.7	10.7	12.0	12.0	16.0	2.7	53.3	14.7	12.0	12.0	16.0	4.0	58.7
Marshall Islands	8.0	2.3	9.0	16.0	2.7	38.0	8.0	6.5	8.0	16.0	2.7	41.2	6.7	7.3	10.0	12.0	6.7	42.6
Micronesia, Federated States of	12.0	6.0	13.8	12.0	5.3	49.1	6.7	8.0	8.8	12.0	5.3	40.8	6.7	11.0	8.8	16.0	10.7	53.1
Mongolia	4.0	5.9	7.5	11.4	4.2	32.9	4.0	10.3	7.9	12.2	4.2	38.6	6.7	10.3	7.9	12.0	7.1	43.9
Myanmar	6.7	11.7	4.5	7.8	2.7	33.3	6.7	12.9	5.0	7.8	2.7	35.0	8.0	13.4	3.4	10.7	5.3	40.8
Nauru	8.0	2.3	7.5	8.0	5.3	31.2	9.3	13.0	10.0	8.0	5.3	45.7	10.7	8.5	10.0	16.0	17.3	62.5
Nepal	4.0	11.3	6.0	5.2	2.0	28.6	4.0	10.8	6.8	4.4	2.0	28.0	5.3	11.3	6.0	10.7	4.0	37.3
New Zealand	20.0	12.6	18.8	10.8	17.9	80.1	20.0	15.6	20.0	7.6	19.0	82.1	20.0	15.6	18.8	17.3	19.7	91.3
Pakistan	4.0	13.9	6.0	4.0	3.8	31.8	4.0	9.5	7.5	4.0	3.8	28.8	5.3	11.5	4.5	6.7	4.7	32.7
Palau	12.0	2.3	6.3	12.0	5.3	37.9	17.3	8.0	17.5	10.8	5.3	59.0	18.7	9.0	17.5	14.7	12.0	71.8
Papua New Guinea	4.0	13.9	7.9	12.8	3.5	42.1	4.0	8.6	8.0	13.8	2.1	36.4	4.0	9.6	7.9	13.3	4.7	39.5
Philippines	8.0	13.3	7.0	7.0	5.2	40.5	8.0	10.9	7.9	4.0	4.2	35.0	9.3	11.4	5.0	8.0	6.6	40.4
Samoa	16.0	6.0	11.3	8.0	6.4	47.6	16.0	7.3	15.0	4.6	5.7	48.6	16.0	8.0	11.3	13.3	5.4	54.0
Singapore	20.0	9.8	18.8	5.4	10.1	64.0	20.0	18.3	18.8	5.6	10.5	73.1	20.0	18.3	18.8	14.7	11.3	82.9
Solomon Islands	6.7	9.8	7.5	18.4	2.7	45.0	6.7	8.3	12.5	18.6	2.7	48.8	5.3	8.3	8.0	14.7	13.3	49.7
Sri Lanka	13.3	12.4	8.8	4.0	7.1	45.5	13.3	9.9	10.0	4.0	7.1	44.3	13.3	12.4	10.0	8.0	7.7	51.4
Taipei,China	14.7	10.0	15.0	12.0	12.7	64.3	13.3	13.3	13.8	4.2	13.6	58.2	14.7	14.7	12.5	9.3	16.4	67.6
Tajikistan	9.3	14.5	8.8	7.0	3.7	43.3	9.3	8.8	11.3	8.2	8.6	46.1	9.3	9.3	9.0	12.0	4.3	43.8
Thailand	10.7	11.5	12.5	4.0	8.5	47.2	10.7	13.7	11.3	4.0	8.3	47.9	13.3	15.7	6.8	8.0	10.6	54.4
Timor-Leste	5.3	10.0	7.0	7.4	2.7	32.4	5.3	8.5	8.0	8.2	2.7	32.7	4.0	9.5	7.0	6.7	14.7	41.8
Tonga	16.0	2.3	11.3	8.0	5.6	43.2	14.7	5.0	8.8	6.4	5.6	40.4	16.0	5.0	8.8	8.0	5.2	42.9
Turkmenistan	8.0	11.3	10.0	7.2	5.9	42.5	9.3	11.4	11.0	8.0	5.1	44.8	12.0	14.4	14.6	8.0	5.1	54.1
Tuvalu	14.7	2.3	9.0	8.0	2.7	36.7	14.7	12.0	13.5	8.0	2.7	50.8	16.0	8.0	15.0	16.0	5.3	60.3
Uzbekistan	9.3	10.7	12.5	5.6	6.0	44.1	9.3	9.4	12.5	7.0	6.0	44.2	12.0	10.4	12.5	8.0	5.9	48.8
Vanuatu	6.7	2.3	7.5	18.0	3.1	37.6	6.7	8.0	10.0	13.4	1.5	39.6	5.3	8.3	9.0	14.7	4.7	42.0
Viet Nam	9.3	10.5	3.0	5.4	5.8	34.1	8.0	11.1	6.0	4.0	4.9	33.9	10.7	12.6	5.0	5.3	6.6	40.2

Source: ADB .

Table A3.7: Differences in Scores

Economy	Changes between 2013 published and 2013 adjusted						Changes between 2016 and 2013 adjusted						Changes between 2016 and 2013 (published)					
	KD1 diff	KD2 diff	KD3 diff	KD4 diff	KD5 diff	NWSI	KD1 diff	KD2 diff	KD3 diff	KD4 diff	KD5 diff	NWSI	KD1 diff	KD2 diff	KD3 diff	KD4 diff	KD5 diff	NWSI
	20	20	20	20	20	100	20	20	20	20	20	100	20	20	20	20	20	100
Afghanistan	0	2	0	0	0	2	0	0	0	−1	1	0	0	2	0	−1	1	2
Armenia	−1	−2	4	0	5	6	3	2	−1	5	−1	8	1	0	3	5	4	14
Australia	0	5	0	0	0	5	0	0	0	4	−1	3	0	5	0	4	−1	9
Azerbaijan	0	0	3	0	−1	2	4	−1	0	3	2	8	4	0	3	3	1	10
Bangladesh	0	3	0	0	−2	1	3	2	2	1	2	10	3	5	2	1	1	11
Bhutan	0	3	−1	−2	0	0	3	0	−1	5	3	9	3	3	−2	3	3	9
Brunei Darussalam	1	8	−1	−4	0	4	0	0	2	9	3	14	1	8	1	4	3	18
Cambodia	0	4	1	1	−2	4	3	−1	0	2	3	6	3	3	1	2	1	10
China, People's Republic of	1	−1	0	1	−3	−2	4	3	2	2	7	18	5	2	2	3	3	15
Cook Islands	−3	−1	2	0	0	−1	0	1	3	4	9	17	−3	1	5	4	9	16
Fiji	−3	0	6	3	−4	3	1	0	−1	3	8	12	−1	0	5	7	4	15
Georgia	−1	0	0	−1	1	−2	4	1	−1	5	1	9	3	0	−1	4	2	8
Hong Kong, China	1	1	−1	0	3	4	0	0	0	0	−1	−1	1	1	−1	0	3	3
India	0	0	1	0	−1	0	0	2	−1	1	2	4	0	2	0	1	1	4
Indonesia	0	0	0	0	−1	−1	1	2	1	4	2	9	1	1	1	4	1	8
Japan	0	0	0	1	2	3	0	1	−3	6	2	6	0	1	−3	7	3	9
Kazakhstan	1	0	3	1	1	7	4	0	1	4	−1	8	5	0	4	5	0	15
Kiribati	0	4	1	0	−5	1	0	1	2	−1	4	5	0	5	3	−1	−1	6
Korea, Republic of	0	4	−2	−4	−2	−4	1	0	3	4	8	17	1	4	1	0	6	13
Kyrgyz Republic	0	0	1	−1	3	2	4	1	0	0	−1	4	4	1	1	−1	2	6
Lao People's Democratic Republic	−1	−2	4	−1	−2	−3	3	2	1	1	−3	3	1	−1	4	0	−5	−1
Malaysia	0	1	1	−2	0	0	1	1	2	7	2	13	1	1	3	5	2	13
Maldives	0	10	1	0	0	11	4	0	0	0	1	5	4	10	1	0	1	16
Marshall Islands	0	4	−1	0	0	3	−1	1	2	−4	4	1	−1	5	1	−4	4	5
Micronesia, Federated States of	−5	2	−5	0	0	−8	0	3	0	4	5	12	−5	5	−5	4	5	4
Mongolia	0	4	0	1	0	6	3	0	0	0	3	5	3	4	0	1	3	11
Myanmar	0	1	1	0	0	2	1	1	−2	3	3	6	1	2	−1	3	3	7
Nauru	1	11	3	0	0	15	1	−5	0	8	12	17	3	6	3	8	12	31
Nepal	0	−1	1	−1	0	−1	1	1	−1	6	2	9	1	0	0	5	2	9
New Zealand	0	3	1	−3	1	2	0	0	−1	10	1	9	0	3	0	7	2	11
Pakistan	0	−4	2	0	0	−3	1	2	−3	3	1	4	1	−2	−2	3	1	1
Palau	5	6	11	−1	0	21	1	1	0	4	7	13	7	7	11	3	7	34
Papua New Guinea	0	−5	0	1	−1	−6	0	1	0	0	3	3	0	−4	0	1	1	−3
Philippines	0	−2	1	−3	−1	−5	1	1	−3	4	2	5	1	−2	−2	1	1	0
Samoa	0	1	4	−3	−1	1	0	1	−4	9	0	5	0	2	0	5	−1	6
Singapore	0	8	0	0	0	9	0	0	0	9	1	10	0	8	0	9	1	19
Solomon Islands	0	−1	5	0	0	4	−1	0	−5	−4	11	1	−1	−1	1	−4	11	5
Sri Lanka	0	−2	1	0	0	−1	0	3	0	4	1	7	0	0	1	4	1	6
Taipei,China	−1	3	−1	−8	1	−6	1	1	−1	5	3	9	0	5	−3	−3	4	3
Tajikistan	0	−6	3	1	5	3	0	1	−2	4	−4	−2	0	−5	0	5	1	1
Thailand	0	2	−1	0	0	1	3	2	−5	4	2	6	3	4	−6	4	2	7
Timor-Leste	0	−2	1	1	0	0	−1	1	−1	−2	12	9	−1	−1	0	−1	12	9
Tonga	−1	3	−3	−2	0	−3	1	0	0	2	0	3	0	3	−3	0	0	0
Turkmenistan	1	0	1	1	−1	2	3	3	4	0	0	9	4	3	5	1	−1	12
Tuvalu	0	10	5	0	0	14	1	−4	2	8	3	10	1	6	6	8	3	24
Uzbekistan	0	−1	0	1	0	0	3	1	0	1	0	5	3	0	0	2	0	5
Vanuatu	0	6	3	−5	−2	2	−1	0	−1	1	3	2	−1	6	2	−3	2	4
Viet Nam	−1	1	0	−1	−1	0	3	2	−1	1	2	6	1	2	2	0	1	6
	−6	80	55	−29	−8	94	63	34	−11	148	129	351	57	110	43	118	121	446

Source: ADB.

Table A3.8: Count Table Differences in Scores

	Changes between 2013 published and 2013 adjusted						Changes between 2016 and 2013 adjusted						Changes between 2016 and 2013 (published)					
	KD1 diff	KD2 diff	KD3 diff	KD4 diff	KD5 diff	NWSI	KD1 diff	KD2 diff	KD3 diff	KD4 diff	KD5 diff	NWSI	KD1 diff	KD2 diff	KD3 diff	KD4 diff	KD5 diff	NWSI
Up 4 points and more	1	13	7	0	2	13	6	0	1	24	11	38	7	16	7	20	11	39
Up 3 points	0	5	5	1	2	4	10	4	2	4	9	4	8	5	5	6	8	2
Up 2 points	0	3	2	0	1	7	0	8	7	3	10	1	0	6	4	2	7	1
Up 1 point	6	5	13	10	4	4	13	17	3	6	7	2	13	6	9	6	14	2
Down 1 point	5	5	6	6	8	4	4	2	11	2	5	1	5	3	3	4	4	1
Down 2 points	0	5	1	3	5	2	0	0	2	1	0	1	0	2	3	0	0	0
Down 3 points	2	0	1	3	1	3	0	0	3	0	1	0	1	0	3	2	0	1
Down 4 points and more	1	3	1	4	2	5	0	2	4	2	1	0	1	2	2	2	1	0

Source: ADB.

7 Comparison of Key Dimensions and National Water Security Index Results Based on Indices (1–5)

AWDO distinguishes five stages of development in national water security from hazardous (stage 1) to model (stage 5). Table 2 of the main text describes these stages. They are directly related to the score of the key dimensions and the NWSI. This section describes the changes in stages (index) for the three cases: AWDO 2013 (as published), AWDO 2013 adjusted, and AWDO 2016. The standard banding (see chapter 9 of the main text) is applied for the NWSI and all key dimensions—and not the individual bandings for the key dimensions as used by the KD teams. This means that the AWDO 2013 index given in Tables A3.9 and A3.10 are (slightly) different from the ones in the published AWDO 2013 report. The basic data about these stages are given in the tables. The setup of these tables is the same as in the previous section.

A comparison is made by analyzing how many economies are in the various stages for the three cases. The result of that analysis is given in Figure A3.1 for the five key dimensions and Figure A3.2 for the NWSI. Comparing the middle column with the left column shows the impact of the changed methodology on the number of economies in the five stages. Comparing the right column with the left column shows the progress that is made by the economies in moving up (or down) in stage. The total number of economies is 48.

Figure A3.1 confirms the conclusions from the previous sections on the impacts of the adjusted methodology:

- The impacts on KD1 and KD5 are minor.
- KD2 and KD3 show a somewhat more positive picture (e.g., fewer economies in stage 1).
- KD4 is more negative (more economies in stage 1).

The conclusions of the comparison between AWDO 2016 and AWDO 2013 (adjusted) are the following:

- KD1, KD2, KD4, and KD5 show improvements (fewer economies in stages 1 and 2).
- KD3 is not really improving.

Figure A3.2 gives the same information for the NWSI. NWSI is the sum of the key dimension scores, which means that the positive and negative changes are evened out to some extent. This also explains why the impact of the adjusted methodology is very limited. The improvement between AWDO 2013 and AWDO 2016 are clear with fewer economies in stage 1 and more economies in stage 3.

Table A3.9: National Water Security Stages for the Three Asian Water Development Outlook Cases

Economy	AWDO (published)						AWDO 2013 (adjusted)						AWDO 2016					
	KD1 Rating"	KD2 Rating	KD3 Rating	KD4 Rating	KD5 Rating	NWSI (average)	KD1 Rating	KD2 Rating	KD3 Rating	KD4 Rating	KD5 Rating	NWSI (average)	KD1 Rating	KD2 Rating	KD3 Rating	KD4 Rating	KD5 Rating	NWSI (average)
MAX	20	20	20	20	20	100	20	20	20	20	20	100	20	20	20	20	20	100
Afghanistan	1	1	1	1	1	1	1	2	1	1	1	1	1	2	1	1	1	1
Armenia	4	3	3	1	1	2	4	2	4	1	3	3	4	3	4	2	2	3
Australia	5	3	4	3	5	4	5	4	4	3	5	4	5	4	4	4	5	4
Azerbaijan	2	3	2	1	1	2	2	3	3	1	1	2	3	3	3	1	2	2
Bangladesh	1	2	1	1	1	1	1	3	1	1	1	1	1	3	1	1	1	1
Bhutan	1	2	2	2	1	2	1	3	2	1	1	2	1	3	2	2	2	2
Brunei Darussalam	4	1	4	2	2	3	5	3	4	1	2	3	5	3	4	3	3	4
Cambodia	1	2	1	1	1	1	1	3	1	1	1	1	1	3	1	2	1	2
China, People's Republic of	2	3	3	1	1	2	2	3	3	1	1	2	3	4	3	2	2	3
Cook Islands	4	1	2	3	1	2	4	1	3	3	1	2	4	1	3	4	3	3
Fiji	4	3	2	2	1	2	3	3	3	3	1	2	3	3	3	3	3	3
Georgia	3	2	4	1	3	3	3	2	4	1	3	2	4	2	3	2	3	3
Hong Kong, China	4	3	5	3	2	3	4	3	4	3	3	4	4	3	4	3	3	3
India	1	2	1	1	1	1	1	3	1	1	1	1	1	3	1	1	1	1
Indonesia	1	3	1	2	1	2	1	3	1	2	1	2	2	3	2	3	1	2
Japan	5	3	4	1	4	3	5	3	4	1	4	3	5	3	3	3	5	4
Kazakhstan	2	3	3	1	3	2	2	3	3	2	3	3	3	3	3	3	3	3
Kiribati	1	1	1	1	1	1	1	1	2	1	1	1	1	2	2	1	1	1
Korea, Republic of	4	3	3	2	2	3	4	4	3	1	2	3	5	4	3	2	4	3
Kyrgyz Republic	2	3	3	2	1	2	2	3	3	1	1	2	3	3	3	1	1	2
Lao People's Democratic Republic	1	3	1	2	2	2	1	2	2	1	1	1	1	3	2	2	1	2
Malaysia	4	3	3	2	1	3	4	3	3	1	1	3	5	4	4	3	2	3
Maldives	2	1	2	4	1	2	2	3	3	4	1	2	3	3	3	4	1	3
Marshall Islands	2	1	2	4	1	2	2	1	2	4	1	2	1	2	2	3	1	2
Micronesia, Federated States of	3	1	3	3	1	2	1	2	2	3	1	2	1	2	2	4	2	2
Mongolia	1	1	2	3	1	1	1	2	2	3	1	2	1	2	2	3	1	2
Myanmar	1	3	1	2	1	1	1	3	1	2	1	1	2	3	1	2	1	2
Nauru	2	1	2	2	1	1	2	3	2	2	1	2	2	2	2	4	4	3
Nepal	1	3	1	1	1	1	1	2	1	1	1	1	1	3	1	2	1	2
New Zealand	5	3	4	2	4	4	5	4	5	2	4	4	5	4	4	4	5	4
Pakistan	1	3	1	1	1	1	1	2	2	1	1	1	1	3	1	1	1	1
Palau	3	1	1	3	1	2	4	2	4	2	1	3	4	2	4	3	3	3
Papua New Guinea	1	3	2	3	1	2	1	2	2	3	1	2	1	2	2	3	1	2
Philippines	2	3	1	1	1	2	2	2	2	1	1	1	2	3	1	2	1	2
Samoa	4	1	3	2	1	2	4	2	3	1	1	2	4	2	3	3	1	2
Singapore	5	2	4	1	2	3	5	4	4	1	2	3	5	4	4	3	3	4
Solomon Islands	1	2	2	4	1	2	1	2	3	4	1	2	1	2	2	3	3	2
Sri Lanka	3	3	2	1	1	2	3	2	2	1	1	2	3	3	2	2	2	2
Taipei,China	3	2	3	3	3	3	3	3	3	1	3	3	3	3	3	2	4	3
Tajikistan	2	3	2	1	1	2	2	2	3	2	2	2	2	2	2	3	1	2
Thailand	2	3	3	1	2	2	2	3	3	1	2	2	3	4	1	2	2	2
Timor-Leste	1	2	1	2	1	1	1	2	2	2	1	1	1	2	1	1	3	2
Tonga	4	1	3	2	1	2	3	1	2	1	1	2	4	1	2	2	1	2
Turkmenistan	2	3	2	1	1	2	2	3	2	2	1	2	3	3	3	2	1	2
Tuvalu	3	1	2	2	1	2	3	3	3	2	1	2	4	2	3	4	1	3
Uzbekistan	2	2	3	1	1	2	2	2	3	1	1	2	3	2	3	2	1	2
Vanuatu	1	1	2	4	1	2	1	2	2	3	1	2	1	2	2	3	1	2
Viet Nam	2	2	1	1	1	1	2	2	1	1	1	1	2	3	1	1	1	2
	116	105	109	91	70	96	114	121	123	83	73	99	128	131	116	117	97	115

Source: ADB.

Table A3.10: Difference in National Water Security Stages for the Three Asian Water Development Outlook Cases

Economy	Changes between 2013 published and 2013 adjusted						Changes between 2016 and 2013 adjusted						Changes between 2016 and 2013 (published)					
	KD1 diff	KD2 diff	KD3 diff	KD4 diff	KD5 diff	NWS diff	KD1 diff	KD2 diff	KD3 diff	KD4 diff	KD5 diff	NWS diff	KD1 diff	KD2 diff	KD3 diff	KD4 diff	KD5 diff	NWS diff
Afghanistan	0	1	0	0	0	0	0	0	0	0	0	0	0	1	0	0	0	0
Armenia	0	-1	1	0	2	1	0	1	0	1	-1	0	0	0	1	1	1	1
Australia	0	1	0	0	0	0	0	0	0	1	0	0	0	1	0	1	0	0
Azerbaijan	0	0	1	0	0	0	1	0	0	0	1	0	1	0	1	0	1	0
Bangladesh	0	1	0	0	0	0	0	0	0	0	0	0	0	1	0	0	0	0
Bhutan	0	1	0	-1	0	0	0	0	0	1	1	0	0	1	0	0	1	0
Brunei Darussalam	1	2	0	-1	0	0	0	0	0	2	1	1	1	2	0	1	1	1
Cambodia	0	1	0	0	0	0	0	0	0	1	0	1	0	1	0	1	0	1
China, People's Republic of	0	0	0	0	0	0	1	1	0	1	1	1	1	1	0	1	1	1
Cook Islands	0	0	1	0	0	0	0	0	0	1	2	0	0	0	1	1	2	0
Fiji	-1	0	1	1	0	0	0	0	0	0	2	0	-1	0	1	1	2	0
Georgia	0	0	0	0	0	-1	1	0	-1	1	0	1	1	0	-1	1	0	0
Hong Kong, China	0	0	-1	0	1	1	0	0	0	0	0	-1	0	0	-1	0	0	0
India	0	1	0	0	0	0	0	0	0	0	0	0	0	1	0	0	0	0
Indonesia	0	0	0	0	0	0	1	0	1	1	0	0	1	0	1	1	0	0
Japan	0	0	0	0	0	0	0	0	-1	2	1	1	0	0	-1	2	1	1
Kazakhstan	0	0	0	1	0	1	1	0	0	1	0	0	1	0	0	2	0	0
Kiribati	0	0	1	0	0	0	0	1	0	0	0	0	0	1	1	0	0	0
Korea, Republic of	0	1	0	-1	0	0	1	0	0	0	2	0	1	1	0	0	2	0
Kyrgyz Republic	0	0	0	-1	0	0	1	0	0	0	0	0	1	0	0	-1	0	0
Lao People's Democratic Republic	0	-1	1	-1	-1	-1	0	0	0	1	0	1	0	0	1	0	-1	0
Malaysia	0	0	0	-1	0	0	1	1	1	2	0	0	1	1	1	1	1	0
Maldives	0	2	1	0	0	0	1	0	0	0	0	1	1	2	1	0	0	1
Marshall Islands	0	1	0	0	0	0	-1	1	0	-1	0	0	-1	1	0	-1	0	0
Micronesia, Federated States of	-2	1	-1	0	0	0	0	0	0	1	1	0	-2	1	-1	1	1	0
Mongolia	0	1	0	0	0	1	0	0	0	0	0	0	0	1	0	0	0	1
Myanmar	0	0	0	0	0	0	1	0	0	0	0	1	1	0	0	0	0	1
Nauru	0	2	0	0	0	1	0	-1	0	2	3	1	0	1	0	2	3	2
Nepal	0	-1	0	0	0	0	0	1	0	1	0	1	0	0	0	1	0	1
New Zealand	0	1	1	0	0	0	0	0	-1	2	1	0	0	1	0	2	1	0
Pakistan	0	-1	1	0	0	0	0	1	-1	0	0	0	0	0	0	0	0	0
Palau	1	1	3	-1	0	1	0	0	0	1	2	0	1	1	3	0	2	1
Papua New Guinea	0	-1	0	0	0	0	0	0	0	0	0	0	0	-1	0	0	0	0
Philippines	0	-1	1	0	0	-1	0	1	-1	1	0	1	0	0	0	1	0	0
Samoa	0	1	0	-1	0	0	0	0	0	2	0	0	0	1	0	1	0	0
Singapore	0	2	0	0	0	0	0	0	0	2	1	1	0	2	0	2	1	1
Solomon Islands	0	0	1	0	0	0	0	0	-1	-1	2	0	0	0	0	-1	2	0
Sri Lanka	0	-1	0	0	0	0	0	1	0	1	1	0	0	0	0	1	1	0
Taipei,China	0	1	0	-2	0	0	0	0	0	1	1	0	0	1	0	-1	1	0
Tajikistan	0	-1	1	1	1	0	0	0	-1	1	-1	0	0	-1	0	2	0	0
Thailand	0	0	0	0	0	0	1	1	-2	1	0	0	1	1	-2	1	0	0
Timor-Leste	0	0	1	0	0	0	0	0	-1	-1	2	1	0	0	0	-1	2	1
Tonga	-1	0	-1	-1	0	0	1	0	0	1	0	0	0	0	-1	0	0	0
Turkmenistan	0	0	0	1	0	0	1	0	1	0	0	0	1	0	1	1	0	0
Tuvalu	0	2	1	0	0	0	1	-1	0	2	0	1	1	1	0	2	0	1
Uzbekistan	0	0	0	0	0	0	1	0	0	0	1	0	1	0	0	1	0	0
Vanuatu	0	1	0	-1	0	0	0	0	0	0	0	0	0	1	0	-1	0	0
Viet Nam	0	0	0	0	0	0	1	0	0	0	0	1	0	1	0	0	0	1
	-2	16	14	-8	3	3	14	10	-7	34	24	16	14	10	-7	34	24	16
Up 2 points	0	5	0	0	1	0	0	0	0	8	6	0	0	3	0	7	6	1
Up 1 point	2	14	14	4	2	6	15	12	3	21	11	17	16	22	11	18	13	17
Down 1 point	2	8	3	10	1	3	1	2	8	3	2	1	2	2	5	6	1	0
Down 2 points	1	0	0	1	0	0	0	0	1	0	0	0	1	0	1	0	0	0

Source: ADB.

Figure A3.1: Number of Economies in Various Development Stages for the Key Dimensions

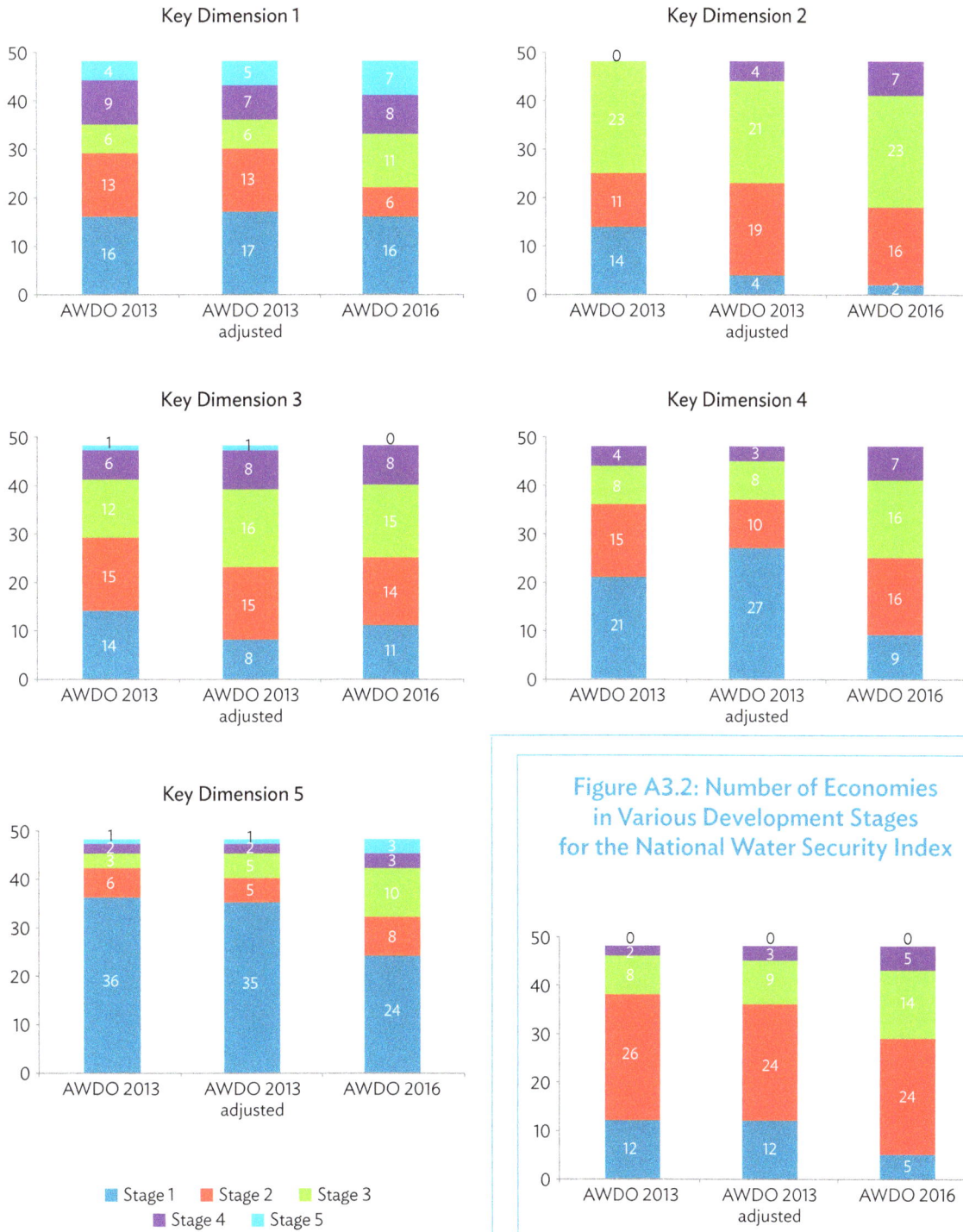

Key Dimension 1

Key Dimension 2

Key Dimension 3

Key Dimension 4

Key Dimension 5

■ Stage 1 ■ Stage 2 ■ Stage 3
■ Stage 4 ■ Stage 5

AWDO = Asian Water Development Outlook.
Source: ADB.

Figure A3.2: Number of Economies in Various Development Stages for the National Water Security Index

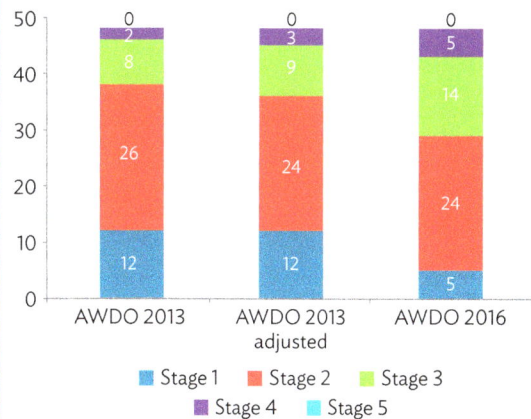

■ Stage 1 ■ Stage 2 ■ Stage 3
■ Stage 4 ■ Stage 5

AWDO = Asian Water Development Outlook.
Source: ADB.

8 Conclusions

The two main conclusions that can be drawn from analyzing the three cases are the following:

- The impact of the enhanced methodology as developed for AWDO 2016 on the outcome of AWDO is not insignificant; and
- AWDO 2016 shows a clear improvement in water security compared with AWDO 2013.

The decision to enhance the methodology was based on identified weaknesses of AWDO 2013, in particular on KD2, KD3, and KD4. Separate studies were commissioned to improve the methodology of these key dimensions. A logical consequence is that the scores of AWDO will change. The AWDO team looked carefully into the cases where these changes are significant and concluded that the new methodology results in a better representation of the water security situation in the countries.

The first conclusion means also that a direct comparison between the results of AWDO 2016 and the published AWDO 2013 is not possible, in particular not for KD2, KD3, KD4, and the NWSI. For this reason, the comparison between AWDO 2016 and AWDO 2013 was based on the adjusted AWDO 2013 results. Care should be taken that this is clear to readers.

The second conclusion is rather firm but at the same time should be viewed cautiously, in particular at the level of individual countries. Although the AWDO team believes in the proposed new methodology, we also acknowledge the limitations in the approach to represent all aspects of water security, in particular at the level of countries with major regional and temporal variations. Data limitations play also a role. This is certainly the case for the small island countries.

APPENDIX 4
Sensitivity Analysis on Double Counting of Urban Water Security Indicators

The five key dimensions each represent one of the dimensions of water security. Although these key dimensions by themselves seem to be independent, the indicators used to quantify them are not completely independent. This is in particular the case for urban water security (KD3) that is described by four subindicators which are also included in other key dimensions: water supply and sanitation (in KD1), floods and storms (in KD5), and river health (in KD4). In some way, this can be seen as double counting of these subindicators in the overall National Water Security Index (NWSI).

The Asian Water Development Outlook (AWDO) is a communication tool. It communicates about the level of water security (at the level of 1–100), the relative position of a country compared with other countries, and the progress countries are making. To investigate the extent to which the issue of double counting influences the first two messages,

a sensitivity analysis has been carried out on the effect of omitting the KD3 scores in the calculation of the NWSI on the absolute and relative position of countries. Results are shown on Table A4.1. It turns out that the level of water security is decreasing on average by 0.2 points with a standard deviation of 2.7 points. Countries with a low KD3 score score higher (e.g., Myanmar, up a maximum of 6 points), other countries score lower (e.g., Turkmenistan, down an extreme 4.8 points). More or less the same applies for the ranking of the countries. The same countries are affected and gain (Myanmar 7 positions higher) or lose (Turkmenistan 6 positions lower) in the ranking of 48 economies. In general, the rankings stay about the same with some countries up or down one or two positions. The overall conclusion of this analysis is that this "double counting" has no major impacts on the message that AWDO is conveying.

Table A4.1: Sensitivity Analysis on Double Counting of Urban Water Security Indicators

Economy	AWDO 2016							AWDO 2016 without KD3							Difference	Difference
	KD1	KD2	KD3	KD4	KD5	NWSI score	Rank	KD1	KD2	KD4	KD5	NWSI score	NWSI score	Rank	NWSI	Rank
Max	20	20	20	20	20	100		20	20	20	20	80	100			
Afghanistan	4.0	8.1	6.0	5.3	4.0	27.5	48	4.0	8.1	5.3	4.0	21.5	26.8	47	−0.6	1
Armenia	18.7	13.1	16.3	9.3	10.8	68.1	11	18.7	13.1	9.3	10.8	51.9	64.8	14	−3.3	−3
Australia	20.0	16.6	18.8	16.0	19.4	90.8	2	20.0	16.6	16.0	19.4	72.0	90.0	2	−0.7	0
Azerbaijan	12.0	12.2	12.5	6.7	7.5	50.8	26	12.0	12.2	6.7	7.5	38.3	47.9	28	−2.9	−2
Bangladesh	6.7	14.1	5.0	5.3	4.2	35.3	44	6.7	14.1	5.3	4.2	30.3	37.9	43	2.6	1
Bhutan	6.7	14.2	9.0	10.7	8.0	48.5	30	6.7	14.2	10.7	8.0	39.5	49.4	26	0.9	4
Brunei Darussalam	20.0	14.3	18.8	14.7	11.4	79.1	5	20.0	14.3	14.7	11.4	60.3	75.4	5	−3.7	0
Cambodia	6.7	12.7	5.6	8.0	4.5	37.5	42	6.7	12.7	8.0	4.5	31.8	39.8	40	2.3	2
China, People's Republic of	14.7	15.3	13.5	8.0	10.4	61.8	17	14.7	15.3	8.0	10.4	48.3	60.4	17	−1.4	0
Cook Islands	16.0	6.8	15.0	16.0	12.0	65.8	14	16.0	6.8	16.0	12.0	50.8	63.4	15	−2.3	−1
Fiji	14.7	11.8	13.8	14.7	11.4	66.3	13	14.7	11.8	14.7	11.4	52.6	65.7	12	−0.6	1
Georgia	16.0	10.5	15.0	9.3	14.0	64.9	15	16.0	10.5	9.3	14.0	49.9	62.3	16	−2.5	−1
Hong Kong, China	18.7	14.7	18.8	12.0	11.9	76.0	6	18.7	14.7	12.0	11.9	57.2	71.5	8	−4.4	−2
India	4.0	12.9	5.6	5.3	5.3	33.1	45	4.0	12.9	5.3	5.3	27.5	34.3	46	1.2	−1
Indonesia	8.0	14.3	7.9	13.3	6.3	49.8	27	8.0	14.3	13.3	6.3	42.0	52.5	23	2.6	4
Japan	20.0	14.3	15.0	12.0	19.5	80.7	4	20.0	14.3	12.0	19.5	65.7	82.2	3	1.4	1
Kazakhstan	14.7	14.8	15.0	12.0	13.8	70.2	10	14.7	14.8	12.0	13.8	55.2	69.0	9	−1.2	1
Kiribati	4.0	7.3	10.0	4.0	5.3	30.7	47	4.0	7.3	4.0	5.3	20.7	25.8	48	−4.8	−1
Korea, Republic of	20.0	15.6	15.0	8.0	15.8	74.4	7	20.0	15.6	8.0	15.8	59.4	74.3	6	−0.1	1
Kyrgyz Republic	13.3	12.3	13.8	6.7	5.8	51.9	24	13.3	12.3	6.7	5.8	38.1	47.7	29	−4.2	−5
Lao People's Democratic Republic	6.7	11.3	8.0	8.0	4.0	38.0	41	6.7	11.3	8.0	4.0	30.0	37.5	44	−0.5	−3
Malaysia	20.0	15.4	15.8	13.3	8.8	73.4	8	20.0	15.4	13.3	8.8	57.6	72.0	7	−1.3	1
Maldives	14.7	12.0	12.0	16.0	4.0	58.7	19	14.7	12.0	16.0	4.0	46.7	58.3	19	−0.3	0
Marshall Islands	6.7	7.3	10.0	12.0	6.7	42.6	34	6.7	7.3	12.0	6.7	32.6	40.7	39	−1.9	−5
Micronesia, Federal States of	6.7	11.0	8.8	16.0	10.7	53.1	23	6.7	11.0	16.0	10.7	44.3	55.4	21	2.3	2
Mongolia	6.7	10.3	7.9	12.0	7.1	43.9	31	6.7	10.3	12.0	7.1	36.0	45.1	32	1.1	−1
Myanmar	8.0	13.4	3.4	10.7	5.3	40.8	37	8.0	13.4	10.7	5.3	37.4	46.7	30	6.0	7
Nauru	10.7	8.5	10.0	16.0	17.3	62.5	16	10.7	8.5	16.0	17.3	52.5	65.6	13	3.1	3
Nepal	5.3	11.3	6.0	10.7	4.0	37.3	43	5.3	11.3	10.7	4.0	31.3	39.1	42	1.8	1
New Zealand	20.0	15.6	18.8	17.3	19.7	91.3	1	20.0	15.6	17.3	19.7	72.6	90.7	1	−0.6	0
Pakistan	5.3	11.5	4.5	6.7	4.7	32.7	46	5.3	11.5	6.7	4.7	28.2	35.2	45	2.5	1
Palau	18.7	9.0	17.5	14.7	12.0	71.8	9	18.7	9.0	14.7	12.0	54.3	67.9	11	−3.9	−2
Papua New Guinea	4.0	9.6	7.9	13.3	4.7	39.5	40	4.0	9.6	13.3	4.7	31.6	39.5	41	0.0	−1
Philippines	9.3	11.4	5.0	8.0	6.6	40.4	38	9.3	11.4	8.0	6.6	35.4	44.3	33	3.9	5
Samoa	16.0	8.0	11.3	13.3	5.4	54.0	22	16.0	8.0	13.3	5.4	42.8	53.5	22	−0.6	0
Singapore	20.0	18.3	18.8	14.7	11.3	82.9	3	20.0	18.3	14.7	11.3	64.2	80.2	4	−2.7	−1
Solomon Islands	5.3	8.3	8.0	14.7	13.3	49.7	28	5.3	8.3	14.7	13.3	41.7	52.1	24	2.4	4
Sri Lanka	13.3	12.4	10.0	8.0	7.7	51.4	25	13.3	12.4	8.0	7.7	41.4	51.7	25	0.3	0
Taipei,China	14.7	14.7	12.5	9.3	16.4	67.6	12	14.7	14.7	9.3	16.4	55.1	68.9	10	1.3	2
Tajikistan	9.3	9.3	9.0	12.0	4.3	43.8	32	9.3	9.3	12.0	4.3	34.8	43.5	35	−0.3	−3
Thailand	13.3	15.7	6.8	8.0	10.6	54.4	20	13.3	15.7	8.0	10.6	47.6	59.5	18	5.2	2
Timor-Leste	4.0	9.5	7.0	6.7	14.7	41.8	36	4.0	9.5	6.7	14.7	34.8	43.5	36	1.7	0
Tonga	16.0	5.0	8.8	8.0	5.2	42.9	33	16.0	5.0	8.0	5.2	34.2	42.7	37	−0.2	−4
Turkmenistan	12.0	14.4	14.6	8.0	5.1	54.1	21	12.0	14.4	8.0	5.1	39.5	49.3	27	−4.8	−6
Tuvalu	16.0	8.0	15.0	16.0	5.3	60.3	18	16.0	8.0	16.0	5.3	45.3	56.7	20	−3.7	−2
Uzbekistan	12.0	10.4	12.5	8.0	5.9	48.8	29	12.0	10.4	8.0	5.9	36.3	45.4	31	−3.4	−2
Vanuatu	5.3	8.3	9.0	14.7	4.7	42.0	35	5.3	8.3	14.7	4.7	33.0	41.3	38	−0.7	−3
Viet Nam	10.7	12.6	5.0	5.3	6.6	40.2	39	10.7	12.6	5.3	6.6	35.2	44.0	34	3.8	5
	589	588	554	539	454	2,723	1,176	589	588	539	454	2,169	2,712	1,176	−11.3	0
													average		−0.2	
													sigma		2.7	2.7

Source: ADB.

Overview of Databases Used for Indicators and Subindicators

	Subindicator	Sub-subindicator	Unit	Data Source	Year of Data	Reference
KD1	Access to piped water supply	None	%	WHO/UNICEF (JMP)	2014	http://www.wssinfo.org/data-estimates/tables
	Access to improved sanitation	None	%	WHO/UNICEF (JMP)	2014	http://www.who.int/healthinfo/global_burden_disease/estimates/en/index1.html
	Diarrhea DALYs per 10,000 people	None	#	WHO	2012	http://www.wssinfo.org/data-estimates/tables
KD2	Broad economy	Coef. of variation rainfall and storage/TRWR		FAO AQAUSTAT Lit.	2012	Harris et al. (2014); FAO AQUASTAT (2015)
		Total freshwater withdrawal/TRWR	%	FAO AQAUSTAT World Bank	2013	World Bank (2015b); FAO AQUASTAT (2015)
		Storage drought duration		FAO AQUASTAT World Bank, Lit.	2000, 2007, 2013	Eriyagama, Smakthin, and Gamage (2009); New et al. (2002); FAO AQUASTAT (2015); World Bank (2015b)
		Data availability; # points	#	ADB, FAO AQUASTAT, IEA, USEIA, Lit.	2010, 2013	ADB (2015a, 2015b, 2015c); FAO AQUASTAT (2015); Harris et al. (2014); Hoekstra and Mekonnen (2012); IEA (2015); USEIA (n.d.); World Bank (2015b)
	Agriculture	Total agric. prod./total agric. water depletion	$ million/km³	IIASA, FAO, MOD, World Bank	2013	ADB (2015c), FAO (n.d.), IIASA and FAO (n.d.); MOD 16 (n.d.); World Bank (2015b)
		Agric. good consumption / agric. good production	ratio	ADB, World Bank, Lit.	2013	ADB (2015a; 2015b; 2015c); ADB (2015b); Hoekstra and Mekonnen (2012); World Bank (2015b)
	Energy	GWh prod. / water consumption	GWh/km³	IPCC, IEA, Lit.	2006, 2010, 2013	Gerbens-Leenes et al. (2008); IPCC (2012); IEA (2015); Mekonnen et al. (2015)
		Present per capita elec. prod. and add. capacity needed	kWh/cap	ADB, USEIA	2013	ADB (2015a; 2015b); USEIA (n.d.)
	Industry	Ind. GDP / Ind. withdrawal	$million/km³	World Bank	2013	ADB (2015c); World Bank (2015b)
KD3	Piped urban water supply access	None	%	WHO/UNICEF (JMP)	2014	JMP (2015)
	Piped urban water supply access	None	%	WHO/UNICEF (JMP)	2014	JMP (2015)

continued on next page

Table *continued*

	Subindicator	Sub-subindicator	Unit	Data Source	Year of Data	Reference	
KD3	Urban wastewater collected	Empirical data—Wastewater collected	%	GWI	2014	GWI (2014)	
		Derived data—a. Slum population	% of urban pop.	UN	2014	UN (2015)	
		Derived data—b. Access to improved sanitation	% of popul.	JMP	2014	JMP (2015)	
	Flood and storm damage	Monetary damage due to flood and storms	$	EM-DAT	2000-2014	EM-DAT (2015)	
		Urban population	#	JMP	2014	JMP (2015)	
		GDP per capita	% GDP	EM-DAT World Bank	2014	World Bank (2015); ESCAP (2015)	
	River health index		–	ADB	2010	AWDO 2016	
	Urban growth rate	None	%/yr	ESCAP	2014	ESCAP (2015)	
KD4	River health index	Based on model results	0–1		2010	Manuscript in preparation	
		Threat to environmental water security	0–1		2000	Vörösmarty et al. (2010)	http://riverthreat.net/data.html
		Total annual runoff	km³		2000 2010	Warszawski et al. (2013)	Balazs Fekete, CUNY Environmental CrossRoads Initiative, bfekete@ccny.cuny.edu
		Population (per grid cell)	# people	CIESIN	2000	CIESIN, 2011 (gridded data)	http://sedac.ciesin.columbia.edu/data/collection/grump-v1
				IIASA	2000 2010	IIASA, SSP database v1.0 (country population growth)	https://secure.iiasa.ac.at/web-apps/ene/SspDb/dsd?Action=htmlpage&page=about
		Water demand (water withdrawn from grid cell flow)	km³		2000 2010	Flörke et al. (2013); Warszawski et al. (2013)	Center for Environmental Systems Research
		GDP (per grid cell)	$ billion		2000	Nordhaus et al. (2006) (gridded data)	http://gecon.yale.edu (World Bank data for each country provide the basis for this spatially distributed data)
				SSP	2000 2010	Shared Socioeconomic Pathways (SSP) database v1.0 (country GDP change)	https://secure.iiasa.ac.at/web-apps/ene/SspDb/dsd?Action=htmlpage&page=about
		Agric. land use (cultivation/livestock	% area of grid cell	IIASA	2000 2010	Manuscript in preparation	Guenther Fischer, IIASA

continued on next page

Table *continued*

	Subindicator	Sub-subindicator	Unit	Data Source	Year of Data	Reference
KD4	River health index	Agric. production (cultivation/livestock)	Gross value ($)	IIASA	2000 2010	Manuscript in preparation Guenther Fischer, IIASA
	Flow alteration	Proportion of undisturbed pixels where disturbed flow is defined as monthly discharge being within a 20% difference from natural discharge, at least once per year.	%	Lit.	2010	Warszawski et al. (2013); Balazs Fekete, CUNY Environmental CrossRoads Initiative, bfekete@ccny.cuny.edu
	Environmental management	Wastewater treatment	%	Yale	2014	Yale Environmental Performance Index (2014) http://epi.yale.edu/
		Pesticide regulation	%		2014	
		Forest loss since 2000	%		2014	
		Terrestrial protection	%		2014	
KD5	General (for all 3 subindicators)	Exposure population density	#/km^2	ESCAP	2012	ESCAP Online Statistical Database
		Exposure urban growth rate	%	ESCAP	2012	ESCAP Online Statistical Database
		Exposure population growth rate	%	ESCAP	2012	ESCAP Online Statistical Database
		Vulnerability governance (corruption)	index	Transparency International	2014	Transparency International https://www.transparency.org/cpi2014/results
		Vulnerability % people below $1.25/day	%	ESCAP	2013	ESCAP Online Statistical Database
		Vulnerability % Net ODA to gross net income	%	World Bank	2012	World Bank Database (World Development Indicators)
		Vulnerability Infant mortality rate/1,000 births	#	ESCAP	2013	ESCAP Online Statistical Database
		Hard coping capacity pot. investment density		World Bank	2014	World Bank Database (World Development Indicators)
		Soft coping capacity literacy ratio	%	CIA	2015 est.	CIA World Factbook
		Soft coping capacity education (enrolment ratio)	%	UNDP	2014	UNDP Human Development Report
		Soft coping capacity Information (TV/1,000 inh.)	#	NationMaster	2003	NationMaster.com Australia

continued on next page

Table *continued*

	Subindicator	Sub-subindicator	Unit	Data Source	Year of Data	Reference
KD5	General (for all 3 subindicators)	Soft coping capacity information (mobile/100 inh.)	#	UNSD	2013	Millennium Development Goals Database (United Nations Statistics Division)
		Soft coping capacity economic growth/ gross domestic saving		World Bank	2013	World Bank Database (World Development Indicators)
	Floods and windstorms	Deforestation rate	%	FAO	2005–2010	FAO - Global Forest Resources Assessment 2010
		Reservoir capacity per area	m³/km²	World Bank, GWSP	2012	Total Dam or Reservoir Capacity: Global Reservoir and Dam (GRanD) Database Land Area: World Bank (World Development Indicators)
	Drought	Agricultural part of GDP	%	World Bank	2014	World Bank Database (World Development Indicators)
		Reservoir capacity per area	m³/km²	World Bank, GWSP	2012	Total Dam or Reservoir Capacity: Global Reservoir and Dam (GRanD) Database Land Area: World Bank World Development Indicators
	Storm surge and coastal flooding	Population proportion living in area below 5m	%	World Bank	2000	World Bank Database (World Development Indicators)
		Infrastructure (paved road density)		CIA	2006–2015	CIA World Factbook

ADB = Asian Development Bank, AQUASTAT = FAO's Information System on Water and Agriculture, AWDO = Asian Water Development Outlook, CIA = US Central Intelligence Agency, CIESIN = Center for International Earth Science Information Network, CUNY = City University of New York, DALY = disability-adjusted life year, EM-DAT = International Disasters Database, ESCAP = Economic and Social Commission for Asia and the Pacific, FAO = Food and Agriculture Organization of the United Nations, GDP = gross domestic product, GWh = gigawatt-hour, GWI = Global Water Intelligence, GWSP = Global Water System Project, IEA = International Energy Agency, IIASA = International Institute for Applied Systems Analysis, IPCC = Intergovernmental Panel on Climate Change, JMP = Joint Monitoring Programme for Water Supply and Sanitation, km² = square kilometer, km³ = cubic kilometer, kWh = kilowatt-hour, m = meter, MOD16 = MODIS global evapotranspiration project, m³ = cubic meter, ODA = official development assistance, SSP = Shared Socioeconomic Pathways, TRWR = total renewable water resources, UN = United Nations, UNICEF = United Nations Children's Emergency Fund, UNSD = United Nations Statistics Division, USEIA = United States Energy Information Administration, WHO = World Health Organization, yr = year.